Another Silenced Trauma

Twelve Feminist Therapists and Activists Respond to One Woman's Recovery From War

Another Silenced Trauma

Twelve Feminist Therapists and Activists Respond to One Woman's Recovery From War

Edited by
Esther D. Rothblum and Ellen Cole

Another Silenced Trauma: Twelve Feminist Therapists and Activists Respond to One Woman's Recovery From War was originally published as *A Woman's Recovery From the Trauma of War: Twelve Responses From Feminist Therapists and Activists* in 1986 by The Haworth Press, Inc. It has also been published as *Women & Therapy,* Volume 5, Number 1, Spring 1986.

Harrington Park Press
New York • London

ISBN 0-918393-29-9

Published by

Harrington Park Press, Inc., 28 East 22 Street, New York, New York 10010-6194.
EUROSPAN/Harrington, 3 Henrietta Street, London WC2E 8LU England.

Harrington Park Press, Inc., is a subsidiary of The Haworth Press, Inc., 28 East 22 Street, New York, New York 10010-6194.

Another Silenced Trauma: Twelve Feminist Therapists and Activists Respond to One Woman's Recovery From War was originally published as *A Woman's Recovery From the Trauma of War: Twelve Responses From Feminist Therapists and Activists* in 1986 by The Haworth Press, Inc. It has also been published as *Women & Therapy,* Volume 5, Number 1, Spring 1986.

Cover design by Marshall Andrews.

Library of Congress Cataloging in Publication Data

Woman's recovery from the Trauma of War.
  Another silenced trauma.

  Reprint. Originally published as: A Woman's recovery
from the Trauma of War. New York : Haworth Press, 1986.
  Includes bibliographies.
  1. Post-traumatic stress disorder—Treatment—Case
studies. 2. Feminist therapy—Case studies. 3. Vietnam
Conflict, 1961–1975—Psychological aspects—Case
studies. I. Rothblum, Esther D. II. Cole, Ellen.
III. Title. [DNLM: 1. Military Nursing—case studies.
2. Stress Disorders, Post-Traumatic—therapy—case
studies. WM 184 W872 1986a]
RC552.P67W66   1986   616.85'212   86-9841
ISBN 0-918393-29-9

CONTENTS

EDITORIAL STATEMENT—NEW CO-EDITORS   1
Esther D. Rothblum
Ellen Cole

INTRODUCTION TO THE SPECIAL ISSUE   3
Esther D. Rothblum
Ellen Cole

Dien Bien Phu   5
Adrienne Rich

Ruth: A Case Description   7

From Alienation to Connection: Feminist Therapy
With Post-Traumatic Stress Disorder   13
Laura S. Brown

Reflections of an Experiential Feminist Therapist   27
Marcia Hill

A Piece of the World: Some Thoughts About Ruth   33
Binnie C. Klein

Re-Evaluation Counseling: A Self-Help Model
for Recovery From Emotional Distress   41
Phyllis Bronstein

Post-Traumatic Stress Disorder in a Vietnam Nurse:
Behavioral Analysis of a Case Study   55
Patricia A. Resick

Perspective of a Sex Therapist   67
Lorna J. Sarrel

Alcoholism First   71
     Michelle Clark

The Interplay of Individual Psychodynamics
    and the Female Experience: A Case Study   77
     Amy B. Ryberg

The Diagnostic Approach: The Usefulness of the
    DSM-III and Systematic Interviews in Treatment
    Planning   91
     Karen John

Perspectives of a Pastoral Counselor   101
     Beth Adamson

Propping Up the Patriarchy: The Silenced Soldiering
    of Military Nurses   107
     Joy A. Livingston
     Joanna M. Rankin

Response From "Ruth"   121

R. LORRAINE COLLINS, PhD: I received my PhD from Rutgers University in 1980 after which I completed a two-year research post doc at the University of Washington. I am currently at SUNY at Stony Brook where I teach and do research on cognitive and social aspects of alcohol abuse. I am also interested in commonalities across addictive behaviors and in the role of alcohol in aggression against women (physical and sexual abuse).

VIRGINIA DONOVAN, PhD: I have a PhD in psychology and am a psychotherapist. Since 1971 I have been a member of the Women's Mental Health Collective, a not-for-profit clinic in Somerville, MA. Our approach to psychotherapy has been informed by our awareness that individual, couple, and family problems can only be understood in the context of broader social issues. My particular area of interest is understanding the implications of emerging feminist psychological theories of development for the practice of therapy.

IRIS FODOR, PhD: Received PhD in Clinical Psychology at Boston University, 1965. Training in child and adult clinical; Chair: NYU (SEHNAP) Women's Studies Commission (1984-85), Professor and trainer of Psychologists for the Schools; Clinical supervisor. Writer, lecturer and practitioner of Cognitive Behavior Therapy, Women's Issues and Mental Health, Assertiveness, the integration of CBT and Gestalt Therapy.

VIOLET FRANKS, PhD: I am a behaviorally oriented, non-sexist therapist particularly interested in problems which affect women. I have a private practice and also am employed in an inpatient psychiatric hospital. I edit a series for Springer Press entitled "Focus on Women."

MIRIAM GREENSPAN, MEd: I have been a feminist therapist in private practice in the Boston area for the past eleven years. I work primarily with women and couples—both heterosexual and homosexual—between the ages of 20 and 50. I also enjoy working with men. I have been involved in teaching, supervising and consulting as well as giving talks on the subject of women and therapy throughout the United States. In the past few years I have extended my consultation services to include workshops on gender relations in high tech industry. My first book *A New Approach to Women and Therapy,* was published by McGraw-Hill in 1983.

JUDITH HERMAN, MD: I received my MD degree from Harvard Medical School and my training in general and community psychiatry at Boston University Medical Center. For the past 14 years I have been a member of the Women's Mental Health Collective, together with Virginia Donovan and Michelle Clark. I am also Assistant Clinical Professor of Psychiatry at Harvard Medical School. My first book, *Father-Daughter Incest,* was published by Harvard University Press in 1981. Both my writing and my clinical work continue to focus on issues of violence in sexual and domestic life.

MARCIA HILL, EdD: My training at Rutgers focused mainly on children and systems, but my work as a psychologist has included a little of everything, from consulting in a variety of settings to therapy and teaching. From this range, I've gradually chosen clinical work, which I continue to find absorbing and endlessly instructive. I now work primarily with women as a feminist therapist in a full time private practice. I am also involved with a local shelter for battered women. My professional interests include the political aspects of therapy, experiential therapy, violence against women, and the nature of the change process.

SHERE D. HITE, MA, is author/researcher of *The Hite Reports,* published 1976 (MacMillan) and 1981 (Knopf), and the forthcoming final Hite Report, to be published 1985 by Knopf. She has been published in 17 countries, and lectured in universities in the U.S. and around the world on women's sexuality and the place of women in history. She has addressed many academic societies, including keynote speeches, to the American Assn. of Sex Educators, Counselors and Therapists, the American Psychological Association, the American Historical Association, the World Congress of Sexology, and others.

MARGARET A. KINGDON, PhD: I earned my PhD in 1974 from the University of Maryland. Currently, I am a feminist psychotherapist in private practice in the Washington, D.C. area where I work with adult women who have a wide variety of concerns including depression, sexuality issues, separation and divorce, sexual abuse, and career and life-style changes. I am also a training consultant and conduct workshops and seminars in areas such as communication skills, women in management, stress management, time management, and career development.

JEAN LATHROP, MA: The first seven years of my adulthood were spent at home trying to be the perfect wife and mother and regarding other women as only competition for the goodies of a patriarchal society. When this life approach failed to work, I went to work, back to school, began co-counseling and joined a women's group. From then on my work (paid and unpaid) became increasingly centered on working with women in educational, therapeutic, and political settings. Currently I teach (women's studies) and counsel in an adult degree program whose primary population is women in transition and am chair of the university status of women committee.

BARBARA MILLER, PhD: Born and grew up in New York City. Went to Sarah Lawrence College and then earned a PhD from Columbia University in 1961. Have had an individual psychology practice for approximately 23 years in the New York area as well as Denver, Colorado, Washington, D.C., and currently Burlington. Specialty areas include: women's self-esteem and coping, adolescence and ethnic minority concerns and stress. Married with 3 children.

JEAN BAKER MILLER, MD, is Clinical Professor of Psychiatry at Boston University School of Medicine and Scholar-in-Residence at the Stone Center, Wellesley College. A recipient of the Rockefeller Foundation Humanities Fellowship, she has written *Toward a New Psychology of Women* (1976) and edited *Psychoanalysis and Women* (1973), as well as numerous articles on depression, dreams and the psychology of women. Fellow of American Psychiatric Association, American Orthopsychiatric Association, American Academy of Psychoanalysis, and have been a member of the board of trustees of the last two. Member, consultant to, and teacher of several womens' groups.

NICOLA MORRIS, MA: I am a teacher and advisor at Goddard College, a small progressive school in Central Vermont. I teach Feminist Studies, Literature, and writing. Many of my students are women who are studying and questioning their own lives and placing their experiences in a political context. I work with women who are seeking to develop a strong sense of self, women who want to find and develop their own power. I have an abiding interest in the barriers that women have to overcome in order to write.

PATRICIA A. RESICK, PhD: I earned my PhD in 1976 at the University of Georgia. After graduating I took a position as an Assistant Professor at the University of South Dakota. In 1980 I was promoted to Associate Professor. After a year as a visiting Associate Professor at the Medical University of South Carolina, I took a position as an Associate Professor at the University of Missouri-St. Louis. My area of research is reactions to victimization, and trauma and therapy of victims.

JILL V. RICHARD, MSW, MA, is currently a Psychiatric Social Worker for a public school system, south of Boston. She provides family, individual and couples therapy, as well as parent education to the families of pre-school and school-aged children. Her background includes administrative and supervisory experience. In addition she has spoken and written on topics related to women and psychology.

MARGIE RIPPER, BA: Currently a faculty member in Sociology at Flinders University in South Australia. Doctoral student in Medical Sociology, with research in the area of the social construction of femininity and illness. Previous research interests include women's health—particularly menstrual cycle effects, feminist theory, self-help, and medical education. Teaching experience includes Women's Studies, Sociology & Community Health.

MARILYN SAFIR, PhD, moved to Israel in 1968, where she taught the first course on Behavior Therapy, helped to found the Israel Behavior Therapy Association of which she was the first President. She is currently a Senior Lecturer in the Psychology Department and directs the Women's Studies Department at the University of Haifa. She recently co-edited *Sexual Equality: The Israeli Kibbutz Tests the Theories* (Norwood Press, 1983) and *Women's Worlds—From the New Scholarship* (Praeger Publications, 1985). Her current research interests focus on Sex Roles and Sex Stereotypes as they relate to sexuality, to sex differences in intellectual functioning, and to socialization practices in city and kibbutz, in addition to feminist therapy.

LINDA T. SANFORD is a licensed psychotherapist and the Coordinator of the Sex Abuse Treatment Unit at Coastal Community Counseling Center in Braintree, Mass. She is the author of *The Silent Children: A Parent's Guide to the Prevention of Child Sexual Abuse* (McGraw-Hill, 1982) and she and Mary Ellen Donovan co-authored *Women and Self-Esteem: Understanding and Improving the Ways We Feel about Ourselves* (forthcoming Viking-Penguin paperback, September 1985). In the past 11 years, she has worked with over 600 sexually victimized women and children and also provides training and consultation on a national basis.

JILL MATTUCK TARULE, PhD, is an Associate Professor at Lesley College in Cambridge, Massachusetts where she teaches and directs the Lesley College Weekend Learning Community, an interdisciplinary program for returning adult students. A developmental psychologist, she is completing a collaborative research project and a resulting book: *The Other Side of Silence, The Development of Women's Ways of Knowing* (Basic Books, forthcoming). Her other research, teaching, administration and publications are in adult development with a particular emphasis on higher education as a support for personal and intellectual development. Her undergraduate degree is from Goddard College, her doctorate in Counseling Psychology from Harvard Graduate School of Education. She lives in Plymouth, Massachusetts with a husband, daughter, two dogs, a cat and, unfortunately, a nuclear power plant.

LINDA TERI, PhD, is an Assistant Professor in Psychiatry & Behavioral Sciences and Chief Psychologist in Geriatric & Family Services Outpatient Clinic at the University of Washington Medical School in Seattle. Since receiving her doctorate in Psychology from the University of Vermont in 1980, she has been actively engaged in teaching, research, clinical work and supervision in the areas of depression, geropsychology and non-sexist therapy. Dr. Teri is author of numerous professional publications and is co-author of *Clinical Geropsychology* (with P.M. Lewinsohn, New York: Pergamon Press, 1983), *The Coping with Depression Course* (with P.M. Lewinsohn, D. Autonuccio and J. Steinmetz, OR: Castalia Press, 1984) and *Geropsychological Assessment and Treatment: Selected Topics* (with P.M. Lewinsohn, N.Y.: Springer Press).

LENORE TIEFER, PhD, BOOK REVIEW EDITOR: Born a New York Jew in 1944, the daughter of a high school teacher and X-ray technician. Given an excellent public education, including the renowned all-girls' high school, Hunter. BA in 1965, and PhD in 1969 from University of California at Berkeley—and imagine the effect of Berkeley in the 60s! First job, because I got my degree before the movement hit, teaching psychology at Colorado State University in Fort Collins. Discovered feminism in 1972. Moved to New York, clinical work, medical center life and the joys of a patchwork career in 1977.

ANN VODA, PhD, is a menopause and menstrual cycle researcher. She was educated initially as a nurse and received advanced graduate training in physiology, specializing in reproductive physiology. She has published widely in scientific journals, presented papers at national and international meetings. Her research and writings reflect a feminist perspective with regard to the medicalization of events related to women's menstrual cycle physiology. She is also a member of the Women's Studies coordinating committee at the University of Utah.

SUSAN WOOLEY, PhD: Received BA in Philosophy, Antioch College, 1964; PhD in clinical psychology, University of Illinois, 1969. Since then on faculty of Psychiatry Dept., Univ. of Cincinnati Medical College. Along with husband and collaborator, Wayne Wooley, involved for many years in study of food intake/weight regulation; founded Eating Disorders Clinic in 1974. Major interests have included the prejudices against fatness; physiological bases of overweight and eating disorders; women and body image; experiential, feminist treatment techniques.

EDITORIAL STATEMENT
NEW CO-EDITORS

This issue of *Women & Therapy* marks the beginning of a new and joint editorship. We begin our role as co-editors at the start of the journal's fifth year. As we succeed Betts Collett, founding editor of the journal, we would like to acknowledge her tremendous energy and enthusiasm in creating a journal that combines theory and practice as it addresses the complex interrelationship between women and the therapeutic experience. During our editorship, *Women & Therapy* will remain dedicated to the journal's founding principles developed by Betts and the former editorial board. Thus, the journal will be devoted to descriptive, theoretical, clinical, and empirical perspectives on the topic of women and therapy. Women comprise the overwhelming majority of clients in therapy. Yet, until recently, there has been little emphasis on this area in the training of therapists or in the professional literature. *Women & Therapy* is designed to fill this information void.

The journal focuses on the following range of content areas:

—issues in the process of therapy with female clients;
—problems in living that affect women in greater proportion than men, such as depression, eating disorders, sexual dysfunction and agoraphobia;
—women's traditional and nontraditional roles in society, and how these affect and can be affected by therapy;
—the special needs of minority women, lesbians, older women, and women with disabilities;

—the special needs of feminist therapists;
—effective intervention and alternatives to traditional treatment approaches.

The term feminism refers to more than advocacy of equality, but to a striving for political, social and economic changes in society. Thus, feminist therapy can include intervention as well as prevention of problems in living for women.

The journal is intended for feminist practitioners and for other individuals interested in the practice of feminist therapy. Journal articles will be of greatest interest to:

—feminist therapists and health professionals;
—individuals who educate, supervise, or train therapists;
—individuals in training to become therapists;
—feminist researchers and scholars who are interested in issues confronting women and therapy.

We are excited by the women who have accepted our invitation to serve on the new editorial board. Their names and a brief biographical sketch appear in this issue. Finally, we welcome submissions to *Women & Therapy* from prospective authors.

Esther D. Rothblum
University of Vermont
Ellen Cole
Goddard College

INTRODUCTION TO THE SPECIAL ISSUE

We begin our editorship with a special issue that deviates from the traditional journal format, and that illustrates varying approaches and perspectives that women therapists and activists, committed to feminism, bring to their work. This special issue begins with a case description (in which all identifying information has been altered to protect confidentiality) of a woman prior to her entering therapy—a woman who was a Navy nurse in Viet Nam and a recovering alcoholic. The remainder of the journal issue consists of articles by feminist therapists and theoreticians who were invited to respond to the case description because of their particular areas of expertise and focus.

Thus, our authors include (1) Marcia Hill, an experiential therapist; (2) Binnie Klein, a therapist who has studied Jungian theory; (3) Phyllis Bronstein, a family therapist; (4) Patricia Resick, a behavior therapist who has experience in treating victims of post-traumatic stress disorder; (5) Lorna Sarrel, a sex therapist; (6) Michelle Clark, a staff psychotherapist who works with a variety of people and who has a current interest and expertise in adult daughters from alcoholic homes; (7) Amy Ryberg, a psychodynamically-oriented therapist; (8) Karen John, an expert on the DSM-III; (9) Beth Adamson, a pastoral counselor; and (10) Joy Livingston and Joanna Rankin, who offer a feminist analysis of militarism. Authors were asked to use any format they desired and to respond to any aspects of the case description, as long as they retained a primary focus on their area of expertise. We were intrigued with the variety in both form and content of the articles we received. Clearly, the authors represent diverse theoretical perspectives but share a commitment to feminism and societal change. The initial author is Laura Brown, who is "Ruth's" actual current therapist and to whom we owe much gratitude for her original draft of the case description and for her courage in allowing us to obtain ten other interpretations of this case description.

Most of all, we thank "Ruth" for giving her permission to have the events and emotional experiences of her life reprinted in this journal, for reading the manuscripts prior to their publication and for writing her response in the final article. "It is men who plan, prepare for, conduct, conclude, describe, and define war" (Stiehm, 1982, p. 245). As a woman, "Ruth" represents less than 3% of veterans of the Viet Nam War. This special issue coincides with the 10-year anniversary of the end of the war in Viet Nam. The media has presented women's roles during this war as mothers and wives, casualties and mourners, refugees and resettlers, anti-war demonstrators, and figures of the street scenes of "back to normal" life. The photograph of Kim Phuc as a nine-year-old victim of an accidental napalm strike is reprinted over and over again in newspapers and magazines reflecting on the war "ten years later." Hers is the only female photograph of the "war's principals and bit players" portrayed in *Time* magazine. Of the 23 individuals described by *Newsweek*, only two are female: Gloria Emersen, a war correspondent and Ly Nguyen, who escaped from Saigon as a baby with her parents. Just as women veterans are unacknowledged victims of the Viet Nam War, expected to "recover" in isolation, so women have always been victims of silenced trauma. We admire "Ruth's" endurance in living through her alienation and pain and in beginning to heal the scars of war.

REFERENCES

Newsweek (1985). Special issue: The legacy of Vietnam.
Time (1985). Special section: Viet Nam ten years later.
Stiehm, J. (1983). Women and men's wars. New York: Pergammon Press.

Dien Bien Phu

A nurse on the battlefield
wounded herself, but working
    dreams
        that each man she touches
        is a human grenade
  ●

                        an anti-personnel weapon
                        that can explode in her arms

    How long
        can she go on like this
        putting mercy
        ahead of survival
She is walking
in a white dress stained
with earth and blood
        down a road lined
        with fields long
        given up   blasted
        cemeteries of one name
        or two
    A hand
juts out like barbed wire
it is terribly alone
if she takes it
        will it slash her wrists again
if she passes it by
        will she turn into a case
        of shell-shock, eyes
        glazed forever on the
                        blank chart of
                        amnesia

"Dien Bien Phu" is reprinted from *The Fact of a Doorframe*, Poems Selected and New, 1950–1984, by Adrienne Rich by permission of W.W. Norton & Company, Inc. Copyright © 1984 by Adrienne Rich. Copyright © 1975, 1978 by W.W. Norton & Company, Inc. Copyright © 1981 by Adrienne Rich.

Ruth: A Case Description

Ruth is a thirty-nine year old woman, referred to a psychologist in private practice by a Veterans' Administration Alcoholism Treatment Program.

She had recently completed a course of inpatient alcoholism treatment. Her sobriety had become a catalyst for her to deal with issues related to her service as a Navy nurse in Viet Nam in 1969 and 1970. She had begun to suffer from increasingly intense symptoms of what appeared to be Post-Traumatic Stress Disorder, for which she had self-medicated with alcohol during the period 1970–1983. At the time she entered therapy, she had been sober for three months. She expressed a sense of ambivalence about therapy, but was also quite fearful of the symptoms she was experiencing, and did not feel that her current support systems, which at that time included regular attendance at AA meetings, an after-care group at the VA, and a weekly peer-counseling session with a Viet Nam Veterans' counselor, were helping her to cope adequately with her problems.

Ruth was the oldest of four daughters of a lower-middle class Catholic family, and had attended parochial schools and a Catholic university. She had enlisted in the Naval nursing corps at the beginning of her junior year in college, in order to secure funding to complete her studies as a registered nurse. She described herself as a good daughter, a straight-A student, popular with peers and comfortable with herself during her growing-up years. Reports from her family members that are available from her VA records corroborate this image. Her memory is that the sole difficult aspect of her growing-up years was the issue of her third sister's cerebral palsy, and her position as "junior mother" in relationship to this sister. She remembers her resentment of her responsibility for the care of this sister, and of the attention that this sister drew from the parents. Her preferred method of coping with this resentment, and one that was reinforced in her family, was to withdraw to her room and read. Ruth sees this as a precursor to some of her adult difficulties with the assertive expression of her needs and feelings, as well as a lesson in how to get attention and care. Ruth lived in her family home until her Navy service began, during her twenty-third year. Until the time of her assignment to a Naval hospital in New York in January of 1968, she had a history of high functioning intellectually (graduating first in her class at nursing school from a challenging BSN program, class commander in Naval Women Officers) and socially (history of diverse social activities, leadership award in Officer Candidate School, dating history similar to that of peers from comparable social/cultural background).

All of this stands in sharp contrast to Ruth's experiences and functioning past that point. Her initial experience as a Navy nurse in New York was that of treating severely wounded battle casualities of the 1968 Tet offensive, who were evacuated to the U.S. one- to three-days post-injury. Her patients were severely burned, missing limbs, and often badly infected. This type of patient constituted her normal patient load for the majority of her time in New York. In July of 1969, she was sent to a Naval Hospital in Da Nang, South Viet Nam, which was the primary facility for Navy and Marine Corps casualties, and remained on duty there until April of 1970, when she was reassigned to duty in the U.S.

This Da Nang experience encompasses a number of significant traumatic events for Ruth. She was under constant threat of attack. The hospital received regular, often daily, mortar shelling; and sniper, grenade, and other terrorist attacks on military personnel while off-base were not uncommon. As did other medical personnel in Viet Nam, she worked shorthanded of both other staff and equipment. Most patients remained in this hospital until they either died or were sufficiently stabilized to be evacuated to Japan or the U.S. The opportunity to care for a patient until recovery did not exist. Her patients were severely wounded: whole body burns, traumatic amputations, terminal malaria. In addition to the daily exposure to maimed and dead bodies at work, she often would encounter them while off duty. For instance, she once witnessed the surfacing of the drowned bodies of three airmen who had crashed into the bay, while she sat having lunch with a friend at a cafe that overlooked the water, an incident that has remained a painful memory. The expectation was held by her colleagues that none of them would discuss their feelings about working in a war zone, and there was a norm of using alcohol to facilitate relaxation and recreation during off-duty hours. It was in this context that Ruth had her first exposure to alcohol use.

While in Da Nang, she entered into her first sexual relationship with a married physician. Although she had little prior experience with which to compare it, she felt that the relationship had significant abusive qualities, both sexually and emotionally. She attributes her sticking with it to a combination of naiveté regarding normative expectations for a relationship and her desire to have "someone to depend on and be protected by" in the midst of a chaotic situation. At the time of Ruth's entering therapy, this remained her sole sexually active experience. Although she had been engaged prior to her military service, that relationship had never moved beyond the petting stage sexually, as both she and her fiancé were devout Roman Catholics. The engagement was ended by both parties, with the estrangement attributed to their long physical separation as a consequence of her military service. Ruth also identified her Viet Nam experience as the point from which she began to depart from her religious beliefs, both in practice and in her ability to believe in a caring diety.

Upon her return to the U.S., she was stationed in a naval hospital in California. She began to complain of pain, chills and fever. After two years in which her condition was diagnosed as psychosomatic, including nine months as a neuropsychiatric hospital inpatient, these symptoms were finally correctly diagnosed as being those of pulmonary tuberculosis, with the lesion at the site of the pain. It was during this time period that Ruth began to drink to alleviate the physical pain as well as the psychological problems she had begun to experience during her stay on the NP ward. Upon her discharge from the Navy, prior to the correct diagnosis of her physical symptoms, she began in therapy with a psychiatrist, who also diagnosed her as suffering from conversion symptoms, and who prescribed Valium for her. She reports that she was using forty milligrams of Valium daily within several months, and continued at this dosage during the four years of her treatment with this psychiatrist. She reports that he was aware of

her increasing alcohol intake at the time, as evidenced by a
written list of therapy goals that included "reduce alcohol
consumption," but that he continued to routinely prescribe
the medication, even after her symptoms were correctly diagnosed as those of tuberculosis. She reports that she was actively discouraged in psychotherapy from discussing her experiences in Viet Nam. She entered and dropped out of nursing
graduate school while in therapy, let her nursing license lapse,
and after a period of drifting in and out of low-paying menial
jobs, secured work as a salesperson for a window-cleaning
firm, where she has remained employed until the present. She
withdrew socially and emotionally from former friends and
from all family members except her youngest (by twenty
years) sister, and began to drink on a maintenance basis, i.e.,
upon arising in the morning, continuously in small quantities
during the day, and a large dose at night to induce sleep.

Ruth reports that beginning in late 1982, her alcohol consumption no longer blocked her psychological symptoms. She
had frequent visual hallucinations and nightmares of dead,
maimed, and bleeding bodies, and a recurrent olfactory hallu-
cination of the smell of pseudomonas, a common infection of
burn victims in the hospitals where she had served. She not-
iced increased hyper-alertness to sounds resembling explosions (although this symptom had always been present) and to
the sound of overhead helicopters, which would induce flashbacks to the medical evacuation helicopters of her Viet Nam
service. She became unable to sleep through the night, even
with large doses of alcohol. Her nightmares included a recurrent theme of being sought out and hurt by badly wounded
men she had cared for in Da Nang and New York. She sought
counseling from a peer-support program for Viet Nam veterans, where she was confronted about her alcoholism, and in
July, 1983, entered an alcoholism treatment program from
which she was referred for individual psychotherapy. At the
time she entered treatment, she continued to experience the
visual and olfactory hallucinations, nightmares, night terrors,
and night sweats. She reported feeling chronically anxious,
and would experience cognitive difficulties, and difficulties
speaking when overwhelmed with anxiety. She was actively
suicidal, and was engaging in frequent self-mutilating behaviors, primarily cutting on the back of her hands and her arms

with razors, knives, broken glass, or her fingernails when no tool was available. She reported that cutting herself relieved tension, and allowed her to cry or to sleep. When not anxious, she reported feeling numb and emotionally cut-off. Although she was in regular therapeutic groups—AA and her VA aftercare group—she continued to isolate herself socially and to avoid forming emotional connections with people during or outside of these group structures. She was often tearful, and experienced difficulty controlling her tears in her work setting. Her self-descriptions were extremely self-accusatory; she was uncertain, at the time she entered therapy, whether any of her symptoms were "real," and accused herself of "making them up to get attention."

Ruth's goals in therapy have been three-fold: (1) to reduce and better cope with the intrusive symptoms of her distress; (2) to come to terms with the overt and symbolic meanings of her life experiences since her service in the Navy began; and (3) to maintain sobriety and to recover from her alcoholism.

From Alienation to Connection: Feminist Therapy With Post-Traumatic Stress Disorder

Laura S. Brown

Having now worked with "Ruth" for nearly two years, it is difficult to separate any hypothetical responses from the reality of what did and continues to occur in our work together. I cannot imagine not having the awareness and analysis of feminism and still being an adequate or useful therapist for her. Indeed, a feminist analysis of the role of women in general, women in the military, and women in the Viet Nam war has been the cornerstone of my conceptualizing, and of the places Ruth and I have gone together in our work.

Conducting a differential diagnosis has been crucial in this case. It is extremely common for women with Post-Traumatic Stress Disorder to be misdiagnosed, and labelled "Borderline". This is the case whether the trauma is Viet Nam, as in "Ruth's" case, or sexual or physical assault (Rosewater, 1985). It is extremely common for therapists who are unaware of basic issues regarding women's personality development to assume that the symptoms they observe in women survivors of trauma are signs of serious underlying pathology, rather than the result of the unfortunate mixture of female socialization and traumatic assault. An additional factor in my assessment was the fact that Ruth was also only sober for three months when she first began to work with me; it was initially unclear how much of what I saw was toxicity, how much the damage of the Viet Nam years and beyond, and how much

Laura S. Brown has a Ph.D. in Clinical Psychology, and has been in the private practice of feminist therapy in Seattle, WA since 1979. She is a member of the Steering Committee of the Feminist Therapy Institute, and has written and taught in a wide variety of settings on feminist therapy theory and practice. In addition, she is active within organized psychology in moving feminist therapy into the mainstream of curriculum content in graduate training in clinical and counseling psychology.

core personality. Ruth had already paid the price for being wrongly assessed by a previous therapist, in not having either her Viet Nam experiences or her substance abuse adequately attended to. And as a feminist therapist, I wanted to avoid the trap of pathologizing her for qualities that would have been normal and expectable for a woman of her class, race, and age cohort. In short, I wanted to make appropriate interventions, and I wanted to acknowledge, respect, and validate the woman inside the pain as real, valuable, competent, and sane. As a feminist and as a therapist, good assessment and diagnosis were crucial.

In attempting a feminist-oriented diagnosis, I looked at several factors, beginning with Ruth's history and functioning prior to her Naval service, which was the identified trauma. This presented a fairly benign picture. There was no history of abuse or neglect, no history of difficulty on this woman's part in attaining normal developmental goals, no history of difficulties in interpersonal relationships or identity development. Rather, there is a picture of a relatively normal lower-middle class woman from a devout Catholic family, whose life mirrored the values and norms of that family in many ways. Although a feminist analysis of this setting would uncover a variety of more subtle sources of damage to women, Ruth was nonetheless an individual who had done well and felt good about herself in that context. As she put it in a recent therapy session, "I did so have a happy childhood! I can remember that; that's not a distortion!" In attempting to project Ruth's life had she followed the path set for her prior to her naval service, I hypothesized that she might have sought therapy at some point in adult life, but mainly to deal with issues of assertiveness with intimate others and appropriate expression of anger and criticism, problems that are so normative for women that they are embedded in the sex-role stereotype of "healthy" adult females described by Broverman, Broverman, Clarkson, Rosenkrantz, and Vogel (1970). (Although it is important to note here that I do not see the normative, e.g., usual, nature of these problems as in any way an endorsement of their "normal", or healthy status. Rather, I wish to comment on the high modal rate of their occurrence.) In short, the definition of a personality disorder as a phenomenon beginning in childhood and continuing into adult development did not fit Ruth as I saw her, even with her years of difficulties. Rather, there was a clear demarcation between her functioning prior to her military service, which could be described as at the high end of the range for women of her class and education, and her functioning after that service, which was markedly and progressively dysfunctional for an individual in any context.

A further confirmation of my initial choice of PTSD as the diagnosis has emerged as therapy has progressed. One of the aspects of this case that has been of particular interest to me, given my use of socio-cultural factors in explaining the development of psychological dysfunctions, is that Ruth's extensive involvement in a variety of support groups has had a significant and positive impact on her, rather than leading to some sort of systems split and battle for control between therapists, groups, and Ruth herself. This confirmed even more strongly my sense that she was dealing with post-traumatic issues, rather than core personality deficits.

My rationale for this is as follows. I have come to have the hypothesis that it is not solely the traumatic event that is the stressor and the source of the psychopathology in PTSD. Rather, it is the combination of the stressor, and a series of socio-cultural factors that inhibit appropriate working-through of the emotions related to that trauma at the time of its occurrence. The effect of a "rule of silence" as a complicating factor in the working-through of trauma can be seen in many similar situations where PTSD becomes the diagnosis: concentration camp survival, incest, and battering, for instance, all seem to worsen in their impact when the victims are abjured not to speak about their experiences. As a feminist therapist, I had had ample opportunity to observe the negative synergy of trauma and silence, abuse and secrecy, that would lead women to feel and act crazy, when in fact it was mainly the context in which they were forced to operate that was pathological.

In this case, Ruth found herself faced, not only with lack of support for experiencing and working through her feelings at the time of the traumatic events, but also with definite barriers to doing so. As a well-socialized woman from a traditionally Catholic family, she had learned a model of adult

womanhood that stressed compliance with designated authority in her own process of giving meaning to internal experience. Consequently, the ways that the designated authorities
labelled her experiences were the ones that she would proceed to internalize. If the pain in her chest was called psychosomatic by the Army physicians, then she felt herself to have
no right to experience it otherwise. If told that her emotional
problems were the result of early childhood trauma rather
than Viet Nam, then she would seek in her past for memories
of problems that never were.

The model of womanhood made available to her during her
development was that of the Virgin Mary, a model that emphasized passive resignation in the face of pain, and that es-
chewed assertive expression of anger. Upon confirmation, at
the age of twelve, Ruth chose to take the name of St. Theresa
of Lisieux, a woman whose primary saintly attributes included
her long-suffering patience and early death, as well as a general selflessness. Thus, the "normal" aspects of Ruth's own
development served as pre-existing, internal barriers to the
working-through of feelings in their appropriate context. In
Viet Nam, where there were implicit norms against the expression of fear of one's own death, sorrow at the pain and
suffering of the wounded being treated, or anger at the situation itself, this client's pre-existing socialization as a "good
woman" interacted with those implicit prohibitions to become
a second barrier to her working-through of her feelings in
situ. Her misdiagnosed turberculosis, which led to her being
labelled by the designated authorities, the Army psychiatrists,
as suffering from psychosomatic symptoms and as neurotic,
served as a further lesson to her that her feelings and her
means of expressing them were inappropriate and unwelcome
to others. A final barrier was in her civilian psychiatrist's
explicit injunctions to not talk about her military experience,
and his labeling of that period of her life as not germane to
her problems. This served to effectively teach this woman that
she should not pay attention to her feelings and memories of
Viet Nam, and worked synergystically with her early socialization in such a way that she found herself with little by way
of coping skills when she did experience the onset of the
nightmares and flashbacks. At this point, she began to utilize
alcohol as a coping tool, as well as the Valium that was pre-

scribed in large amounts for her by her psychiatrist. As was true for many other women attempting to speak the truth about their pain, Ruth was chemically silenced by the "helping" professionals she went to. It appears that her attempts to work through her feelings ended at that time, to re-emerge upon her attainment of sobriety in July of 1983.

The social support networks which she joined upon her sobriety all have as a major goal for their participants the validation and expression of internal reality and emotional experience. In AA, for instance, an alcoholic is encouraged to speak the truth about feelings and experience, and to see the avoidance of truth as a step back to drinking. Viet Nam veteran peer counseling gave this client, as other Viet Nam veterans, a setting in which both the memories of Viet Nam, and the feelings in response to those experiences, were shared, accepted, and validated. The VA alcoholism program aftercare group in which she participated for a nine-month period following discharge has a norm of encouraging assertive expression of feelings, based on research conducted at that program that indicated that this emotional openness is essential in reducing drinking relapses.

Thus, were this woman indeed suffering from PTSD, she should experience some relief from her participation in these groups, where she received support to remember, belief in her memories, encouragement to feel and express feelings honestly, and validation of the reasonableness of her feelings about her military experiences and her subsequent life. By the time she entered therapy with me, Ruth had already been participating, to one degree or another, in all of these groups, and reported that her participation in these groups was serving as a catalyst for greater feeling awareness and expression, as well as a dawning belief in the realness of her experiences in Viet Nam and the non-uniqueness of her emotional responses to those experiences. She experienced these support group settings as essential learning experiences in her process of recovery. In short, the aspect of Post-Traumatic Stress Disorder that is related to feelings of alienation and isolation was being alleviated to a noticeable degree for this client by her group participation. Thus, the total diagnostic picture presented by this client seems to confirm a diagnosis of Post-Traumatic Stress Disorder; the longer her recovery, the more clearly her functional inner core emerged. As she began to experience permission to believe herself and to speak the truth about her feelings, the Ruth of pre-Viet Nam days began to be visible again.

A final important aspect of my analysis of Ruth's problems, which moves beyond the issue of formal diagnosis, and into the questions of my philosophy of psychotherapy and assessment, rests in a feminist analysis of her situation. As a feminist therapist, a question that must always figure in my conceptualization of a case is, "How does this person's status and experience as a woman in her culture shape her personality or her psychological dysfunction?" The question of how she is perceived, and thus treated by others, and the question of how she sees herself are powerfully affected by cultural norms and beliefs regarding women and their nature.

In this case, the feminist analysis leads to several crucial issues. The first, which I have already discussed in brief, is the issue of her socialization as a woman in the culture of a lower middle-class, Irish, traditionally (i.e., Pre-Vatican II credal system) Catholic family. Each of the traditional Western religious traditions carries with it certain norms about acceptable behavior in women. Within a Catholic cultural setting, those norms include the development of a quiet, passive, compliant mode of operation, with men as authorities and decision-makers, and women as care-takers and hand-maidens. Anger and active sexual expression are considered sinful; bad things that occur in one's life can be construed as just punishment for sins. A number of feminist commentators from the Catholic tradition (Daly, Warner) observe that a majority of female saints are models of the extremes of the role of the "Good Catholic Woman": they are saintly because they are good victims in the cause of their beliefs. This client's confirmation saint, as previously noted, was one who exemplified the concept of "good woman as suffering woman."

Ruth had described herself as having been a "good girl", a model student, and a willing and active participant in her culture and its norms. It is highly likely that she came to internalize those norms, and to apply them to herself when she encountered the situations of her military service. Consequently, an important aspect of Ruth's therapy has been for me to share with her the information sources that I had had available to me. In this way, she could begin to understand, at a cognitive level, the meaning and impact of having been socialized as she was, and the bearing of those experiences on the problems of her adult life.

A second issue which called for feminist analysis is that of the position of the woman in the military. A common description of the woman veteran, and in particular, the woman veteran of Viet Nam, is that she was "not there". Women veterans' rights to full veteran's benefits were not established until the mid-1960s. Women's military service in Viet Nam was presupposed by many to not carry with it any risk, since, as non-combatants stationed in "safe" areas, there was presumed to be no exposure to battle or the possibility of personal injury or death. Finally, women serving in the military are subject to a series of humiliating and degrading stereotypes of a sexual variety, which seem to fall into characterizations of such women as either whores or lesbians, two groups that are socially stigmatized. Such stigma is used by patriarchal society to retain social control over other women's sexual expression and life choices (Pheterson, 1984). Women serving in the military are often so stigmatized and oppressed. Consequently, an issue that needed attention in therapy was an analysis of Ruth's participation in a devalued occupation in which the existence of risk was high, yet denied, and where both the devaluation and the denial were outgrowths of her status as a woman. An additional factor that we came to explore in therapy was the question of just how vulnerable "Ruth" had been rendered by her socialization to internalizing the stigmatized aspects of her work as a military nurse. My initial theory, which I have seen confirmed in the course of therapy, was that her normative socialization in her culture rendered her quite vulnerable, and that she had in fact taken on the sense of stigma that was assigned to her role as a military woman by the culture at large.

I drew from a wide variety of techniques in working with "Ruth". My behavior as a therapist has been influenced by Gestalt techniques and theories, and by Transactional Analysis. My feminist perspective has led me to take a highly phenomenological approach to the process of understanding human development and change. In intervening and assessing, I constantly ask myself how the experience of reality for this particular individual has led to her unique ways of comprehending and coping with that reality, while, simultaneously, asking how this individual's membership in a particular social class informs or transforms that internal experience of external events. My techniques as a therapist have as a goal increasing the client's awareness of and access to her feelings and past experience, concomitant with a cognitive understanding of how those past experiences inform her current styles of coping and surviving. In addition, I attempt to aid my clients in respecting and understanding their experiences and feelings in the light of their social class memberships, and to avoid using inappropriate standards for judging their behaviors and coping styles. For instance, I avoid using a model of healthy adult functioning that takes only the male gender role as its paradigm of adulthood, or only a Caucasian or middle-class model of coping as a paradigm for appropriateness. Rather, I explore with my clients the norms for their particular class or classes, with a goal of seeing value and meaning in those norms, and of learning to challenge the usefulness of those norms for women without devaluing their own unconsenting participation in them. For Ruth, that has meant an emphasis on bringing memory and feelings into consciousness so that she can examine and make sense of her experiences. In addition, there has been a focus on her learning how her being a woman, a nurse, a Viet Nam veteran, a Catholic, and a college-educated lower-middle class person, all bear on both the experiences she has had, and the meaning of those experiences for her.

An additional and very essential aspect of our work together has been my feminist perspective on how power is defined and shared in the psychotherapy process. Ruth had been badly, almost fatally stripped of her personal power by previous therapy. At times, that powerlessness to define her experience has seemed to both of us to have been almost more traumatic than the experiences themselves. Yet it was clear, upon her entering therapy, that I had more power. This is true in any therapy setting; the relationship is assymetrical, and in many ways must remain so for therapy to take place. How then, to empower Ruth, and to utilize the power of my position as therapist to do that, rather than to further rob her of her personal integrity?

It has been my experience, and I think Ruth's as well, that my empowering of her has taken a number of forms. My willingness to believe her, and to challenge her internalized oppression, which takes the form of her minimization of the abusive nature of her experiences in Viet Nam and thereafter, has been central and on-going. My willingness to share my primary sources with her, and thus not be in charge of information, has also been important as a means of demystifying myself as a therapist.

We have worked with a variety of techniques for enhancing development of feeling awareness. These include gestalt awareness continuum exercises, in which Ruth has learned to more precisely attend to her physical feelings and become more aware of tension or discomfort in her body. Since this client had been anesthetized for a long time by her substance abuse, and early in her sobriety had been able to experience only anxiety, which seemed to act as a barrier to the experience of other feelings or relevant memories, the rationale for focussed feeling-awareness exercises has been to regain familiarity with the physical representations of her emotions, and to thus have better access to feelings as they emerge. A second technique for increasing awareness of emotion and access to memory has been increasing the client's awareness of her breathing. She often holds her breath for extended periods when an emotion or a memory would begin to emerge, in an attempt to block the feeling. The result would be anxiety. Teaching this client to attend to her breathing, and to breathe regularly and normally when emotions come up has been a very important part of aiding her in gaining access to feeling and memory. In addition, from a feminist therapy perspective, it has served to move her into re-owning and revaluing her body and the wisdom that comes from it. Moss (1985) has commented on the importance for feminist therapists of teaching women to integrate body and mind, thus avoiding either an androcentric emphasis on the intellect only, or a stereotyping of a woman as being more body than soul. In attending to her body's wisdom, Ruth has learned to better trust and know herself, and to see how she has always accurately and perceptively comprehended the situations in which she found herself. Unlearning cultural messages to ignore her body leads to greater empowerment.

A second important aspect of intervention has been the validation of her experiences and her reactions to them. A major technique for this has been my active encouragement of her detailed discussion of memories of Viet Nam. I have encouraged her to print and bring into therapy sessions photographs she took during her service there to act as an aide-memoire, and to remind her that the experience did really occur in an actual physical place that is represented in the photos, rather than in her imagination only, as she often has accused herself of "making this all up to get sympathy." As a further reality test, I have asked her to read first-person accounts of service in Viet Nam and its aftermath, in particular, the book *Home Before Morning,* (Van Devanter, 1983) which is a first-person account by an Army nurse, from a cultural background very like Ruth's, who served in Viet Nam, and who wrote of her experiences in the aftermath of her service. This prescription came very directly from the feminist principle that calls on us to validate and connect the realities of women's lives. Ruth found these suggestions helpful, and has expanded upon them herself. About a year into therapy, she came upon a poem by Adrienne Rich entitled "Dien Bien Phu", which speaks with the voice of a nurse in Viet Nam. Ruth has shared the poem with other women veterans, finding it a powerful metaphor for her own internal experiences. Along the same lines as the support for validation from books, I also have supported her participation in the Viet Nam veteran peer-counseling program, and in Viet Nam veteran's action groups, as a means of gaining access to other veterans, particularly women veterans. In the therapy hour itself, validation can be aided and accomplished by verbal interchanges in which I employ active listening, and in which I verbally confront this client's distortions and self-criticisms regarding her experience and her feelings. In addition, I verbally reframe this client's analysis of her experiences in ways that will allow her to be more forgiving of and compassionate with herself. For instance, when she accuses herself of overreacting, I will ask her to consider the symbolic meanings of her experience before evaluating her reaction critically. In examining what a particular here-and-now experience may mean in light of her past experiences, she can accomplish two tasks simultaneously; feeling more valid about her current emotional responses, and becoming more aware of the connections between past and current events, thus increasing her perceived control of her current life. A further means of validating her emotional reactions has been to confront her cognitive distortion regarding appropriate responses to the traumatic events of her military service. By sharing information about women's socialization, and about the impact of her status as a woman in the military on the development of her standards for emotional "appropriateness", this client has been able to become more accepting of her own feelings, and more aware of how she gained the distorted and hypercritical views of emotional expression that she had been using to actively repress her own feeling expression.

Another important aspect of my intervention in this case has been the use of the therapy relationship as a paradigm for the development of relationships in this client's life. One of her common cognitive distortions has been that it was inappropriate for her to want and seek out emotional intimacy with others as a way of coping with her fears and sadness. She had internalized a somewhat counter-dependent, androcentric model of adult autonomy, and used those norms and constructs to criticize her desire for closeness and emotional openness as "weakness" and "dependency". In the therapy sessions, I give verbal permission and support for interdependent behavior. Via bibliotherapy, I have introduced the client to Miller's (1976) model of normal female development in which healthy interdependency, and integration of dependency needs with autonomy are seen as goals of female adult development. I have encouraged her dependent symbolic relationship with me, in which she can allow herself to regress and know that she will be taken care of, while simultaneously encouraging and supporting her development of meaningful interdependent, emotionally intimate relationships with peers. This client can then learn that she can be dependent without being "dependent upon", that she can shuttle between regression and adult functioning, and can be intimate while still autonomous. Even though she may feel dependent at times in therapy, she knows that she can and does depend on others besides me, and that others can and do get support from her. She has been able to have the experience that I believe in, support, and validate her active, adult, expressive behaviors simultaneous with her "little kid" feelings and ways of being. This has been another form of sharing power and empowerment, as therapy has provided a home base in which to practice being fully herself, with all aspects of self acknowledged, respected, and seen as real, not cancelling each other out. This willingness on my part to see and respond to her whole self has been particularly important in our work on issues of anger and separation, which are anxiety-provoking for many women, and for Ruth in particular, given her learning experiences. When very anxious, she has a difficult time speaking, and would, in the beginning of therapy, attempt to minimize her feelings in order to speak, or alternatively, berate herself for being so intensely in a feeling state that she could not be a "good client" and tell me what was happening internally. A very empowering intervention for her has been my ability to "accurately symbolize", to give her a verbal summary of what I believe her to be saying during these dysfluent periods. This has served as reassurance that she is, in fact, not crazy. When I am able to give her feedback that is a coherent encapsulation of what are often disjointed and highly emotional fragments of verbal output on her part, she is able to hear herself, and to work through her anxiety to greater clarity, both verbally and cognitively.

Behavioral and fantasy rehearsal of anger expression has become an increasingly important component of therapy. The rationale for that is that anger is a major emotion that this woman continues in having difficulty identifying and expressing. When an event occurs to which she might reasonably respond with anger, she instead often experiences a constellation of physical symptoms, anxiety, and difficulty speaking and breathing. In sessions, I have verbally encouraged her expression of anger to me, e.g., when I was about to leave on vacation, as well as her rehearsal of expression of anger toward significant others. This rehearsal has nearly always been a trigger for feelings of fear regarding loss and separation. Thus, rehearsal of anger expression has also led back into the issues of validation of memory and experience, and into the cognitive understanding of how here-and-now events are symbolically related to past trauma.

A final facet of therapy has been the development of this client's sense of personal history. By asking her to speak in depth about her growing-up experiences, she has begun to see herself more clearly in the light of that socialization. As she develops a sense of continuity, and of the synergystic, although unfortunate, interaction of her earlier development with her military experience, she has begun to see herself and her reactions as less "weird" and more predictable. Again, I have utilized personal photographs as a reality-test for this client, so that she is able to have a concrete reminder of who and how she was growing up, and how that person was prepared or not for the experiences she had in the military and thereafter. This has had the effect of increasing her sense of self-esteem, and her willingness to see some of her symptoms as "survival skills" rather than as "crazy", highly pathological responses. This has also aided her in reevaluating her distortion that she should have been emotionally prepared to deal with the events of her military service, and has allowed her to see how her active participation in the norms of her family's culture shielded her from experiences that might have prepared her better dealing with the sort of abuse that she experienced, both in the military and afterwards.

The content of any given therapy session is determined by Ruth's needs, in keeping with the feminist therapy principle of sharing power with clients by giving them choice of focus. Both content and process issues are dealt with as they emerge, with the former usually revealing the nature of the latter as a session progresses.

Thus, both for Ruth and for me, the feminist perspective of our work together has been essential and empowering. It has emphasized for me how differently feminist therapy responds to a woman's distress than does a traditional approach, and reminded me, again and again, of how much our theory has to offer to any therapist's practice.

I recently had the pleasure of hearing Ruth's participation in a program at a professional meeting, where she shared her experiences with the audience in an attempt to educate them about the issues and concerns of women veterans dealing with PTSD. She had organized the symposium from among members of her women veteran's support group, many of whom had had experiences similar to her own, both in the service and upon their return to civilian life. I see this as a concrete illustration of where she stands today, almost two years after our work together began. We continue to work together; memories full of anger and pain continue to surface, developmental tasks lost in the years of drinking continue to present their challenges and pitfalls. Yet it is clear that Ruth is more healed and whole. Certainly she is more willing to be the expert on her experiences and their meaning, and to play that role in front of my professional colleagues. That reembrace of power on her part, and her move into the position of her own best authority; those say to me most clearly what a feminist perspective does to transform the meaning of the therapy process.

REFERENCES

Broverman, I. K., Broverman, D. M., Clarkson, F. E., Rosencrantz, P. S. and Vogel, S. R.(1970) Sex-role stereotypes and clinical judgments of mental health. *Journal of Consulting and Clinical Psychology, 34* 1–7.

Daly, M. (1973) *Beyond God The Father.* Boston: Beacon Press.

Miller, J. B. (1976) *Toward A New Psychology Of Women.* Boston: Beacon Press.

Moss, L. E. (1985) Feminist Body Psychotherapy, In *The Handbook of Feminist Therapy: Women's Issues in Psychotherapy.* L. B. Rosewater and L. A. Walker, (Eds). New York: Springer Publishing Company.

Pheterson, G. (1984) Alliance Between Whores, Wives, and Dykes. Paper presented at the Third Annual Advanced Feminist Therapy Institute, Oakland, CA.

Rosewater, L. B. (1985) Schizophrenic, Borderline, or Battered? In *The Handbook of Feminist Therapy: Women's Issues in Psychotherapy.* L.B. Rosewater and L.A. Walker, (Eds) New York: Springer Publishing Company.

Van Devanter, L. (1983) *Home Before Morning.* New York: Beaufort Books.

Warner, M. (1982) *Alone of All Her Sex: The Myth and Cult of the Virgin Mary.* New York: Vintage Books.

Reflections of an Experiential Feminist Therapist

Marcia Hill

I had several reactions to reading the description of Ruth. One was something to the effect of, "Whew, she must be in a lot of pain," tinged with a sort of pleased appreciation for the strength of endurance in this woman. Another thought was, "If I were Ruth, I'd be none too trusting of so-called 'helping professionals.' " My main reaction, though, was "I wonder what this woman will be like?" and in that, I think, lies the gist of my approach to a new client. There is all that data about her, and yet it no more describes what is crucial than the words to a song describe the melody. I'm no worse off for reading the description, I suppose, but also no better off. It doesn't tell me what I need to know. Because the information and resources I need to do therapy are in the client, I will be able to say very little about how I would proceed that is specific to Ruth. However, I can say some things about therapy in general, and then describe possible applications to working with Ruth.

DIRECTION: WHERE DO WE START?

To begin with, what do I need to know? I need to know where the trouble is for Ruth. What is the nature of her pain? What quality of living inside Ruth is not what it needs to be? What I want to listen for, and try to help Ruth grope toward with my questions and reactions, is the essence of her experience of herself, particularly in the area which is difficult. This is

---

Marcia Hill, Ed.D., is a psychologist in full-time private practice in Montpelier, Vt. She is a member of the editorial board of *Women & Therapy*.

different from simply how she feels or what is observably
"wrong" in her life. For example, there may be a closed-down,
heavy, "of course" quality to her description of herself, or a
tone of quiet waiting without hope, or an edge of always-vigi-
lant readiness for attack, coiled like a snake. I don't necessarily
have to know what hurtful things happened to Ruth, or even
what her symptoms are. History or symptoms are significant
only to the extent that the client and I can use them to further
meaning. Of itself, a grocery list of symptoms signifies little.
And historically based conclusions of the "Of course she's
over-responsible, she was the oldest child" sort leave one
wondering, "So what?". Ruth may well come into my office
and begin by discussing her past or the things that she finds
unsatisfying in her current life. But the key to all we would do
is Ruth's present experience of that in her which needs attention. One finds the shape and resources for what is possible
inside the very nature of the trouble.

There is a way in which the worst of any pain is always
stopped movement. The grief which is allowed to weep; the
anger which is welcomed as just, even if not expressed in the
moment; the trouble with one's mother which is appreciated
and looked at with caring curiosity regardless of how awful it
may feel—these things do not bring people to my office. To be
alive is to move forward. To stop that movement is an act of
desperation which carries with it a pain deeper than that of
other feelings: the pain of death. So with Ruth I listen and feel
and watch for a very specific kind of information. Where has
she stopped herself? What is the nature of her desperation?

There is another kind of information I need from Ruth,
which will address the issue of how I might best accompany
her. This is the issue of *how* we proceed (in the sense of
manner or style) as opposed to where or toward what we
proceed. Is Ruth formal or playful? How cautious is she, how
much interpersonal distance feels right to her? What kind of
language (in the broadest sense) does she use; how does she
express herself? What general emotional tone does she con-
vey? The questions are myriad, but it is not necessary to
articulate them, even to myself. I simply allow Ruth to provide the language; I respond to her within that language. This
isn't a change in who I am, but rather a tempering or expand-
ing or fine-tuning of my style based on that of the client. We

are all slightly different with different people: that's the essence of good communication. Therapy should be the best of communications—too much is at stake to do otherwise. In addition to relatively simple matters of style, this also applies to larger issues such as speed and intensity. Timing is critical to good therapy. If I am too eager, I violate what the client has conveyed to me about her need for safety and foolishly disregard the best information we have about what to do next. If I am too careful, I insult and weaken my greatest ally: the client's access to her courage and resources.

OUTCOME: WHERE ARE WE GOING?

Other than information from the client, the single most important factor for me in knowing what to do in therapy is knowing the outcome I want. I don't mean outcome in the sense of specific choices, of course; I have no way of knowing what shape the client's life will take as she changes in therapy. It is not even particularly important to me what she decides about work or relationships or lifestyle. When I think of outcome, I think of a way of being with oneself and a kind of movement which comes out of that. Having a clear vision of these two elements allows me to know when the client and I are moving in the right direction and what needs to be done differently when we are not. Both elements are discussed in greater detail below.

First, there is a way of being with oneself, especially, a way of being with whatever the trouble is in one's life. To think about having any kind of relationship with one's pain presupposes an aspect of self which is not identified with the pain, which can stand outside of the pain and regard it in some way. This is the essence of insight, but insight requires only a neutral stance toward one's difficulty. The kind of relationship with self which is most enabling of change is one that is warmly welcoming: a mother-child relationship, or that of the best of friends. This is more than self-acceptance. It assumes the other's good intentions, appreciates the other's strengths, holds the other's sorrows in deepest sympathy. In a word, this relationship is loving.

Secondly, there is a kind of movement which is made possible in the environment of that loving relationship. This involves a change in the way that the problem is experienced, not simply an adjustment to it or a way of coping with it. There is a change in the basic formulation of the issue, often in surprising ways. A client may find, for example, that her repeated seeking out of abusive relationships carries a certain thrill. On the face of it, this seems self-destructive, even "masochistic". But when we look more carefully at the thrill, it reveals itself as a joy in surviving pain, in proving that her spirit remains alive under the worst of adversity. And then she recognizes that this was the only road to power which was available to her while growing up in a depriving and abusive home. This is a larger perspective which results in a wider range of choices as well as an appreciation for the choices she has made until this point. There is no way, of course, that I can anticipate the specific kind of movement which is right for Ruth, any more than I could have predicted the particular shift in feeling and understanding for the client in the example above. There are, however, characteristics of this kind of movement that I can watch for and use to help shape our progress. One characteristic lies in the timing of the change. Change happens after or while one holds the problem in that caring relationship, not before. Another trait of such movement is that it is fundamentally affirming. In the new light of the change, the client may feel sad about the way in which she had carried the hurt in her life, but she recognizes that she clearly did the best that she could and with the best of motivations. Finally, this movement is a change in the whole sense of the problem, although it may be only one such change in a series. This kind of change makes the situation feel easy, although it may now be even more difficult in practical terms. There is a feeling of lightness or expansiveness. There is more energy. Feeling good is *easier* than feeling bad.

Therapy, then, is simply a process of matching the information from the client about where she is stopped with my own understanding of what forward movement feels like and what is necessary for such movement to occur. I will make some guesses about the form that this might take for Ruth; however, I want to reiterate that there is no way that I can know what Ruth's experience is until she tells me. These are only my imaginings.

POSSIBLE APPLICATIONS TO RUTH

I would guess that Ruth might need some help both with her relationship with her hurt and with finding a way to move it. When I consider Ruth's attitude toward her hurt, I note that she has tried a variety of ways to try to make her pain go away. She has numbed it with alcohol, told it that she didn't believe it was real, and then scolded it for not cooperating by vanishing. She even had the unfortunate "assistance" of a psychiatrist who also tried to make her pain go away by drugging it with Valium and telling it not to speak. Luckily, none of those tactics worked, which is a tribute to the tenacity of her urge to heal. If she had somehow managed to get her symptoms to subside to a tolerable level while leaving the heart of her pain untouched, she would have been condemning herself to a life that was muted and constricted, a life only partly lived because it was without access to a large part of her experience. Ruth's symptoms are her efforts to take care of what happened to her in Viet Nam, to detoxify herself. As such, their intensity is exactly right. As a nurse, Ruth knows that pain is the body's signal of injury. Psychological pain is not different. The fact that she hurts says that she has been damaged, and to a degree reflected by the degree of hurt. People do not manufacture pain unless it is absolutely necessary.

The nature of Ruth's pain is her own knowledge of how she has been harmed, articulated in an internal, bodily way. This is the key to healing that injury. We need to understand what the experience of Viet Nam meant to her, what damage it did to her. While such a traumatic situation would cause anyone to have some kind of difficulty, we each would have a unique reaction depending on the meaning we made—or failed to make—out of that particular experience. What has it meant to Ruth to have witnessed terrible things? Has she found a way to feel comfortable ownership of a life that contains the grotesque contrast of the smell of pseudomonas and the smell of lilacs; can she find comfortable citizenship in a world which contains such contrasts? I would guess that Ruth survived two years which were saturated with the smell of death by closing down her perceptions and responsiveness in a general way. Almost anyone who had lived through Viet Nam would have felt terrified and powerless, but what specific shape have these feelings taken in Ruth? And what do these feelings need? Ruth's bad feelings are the part of her that knows what feeling good would be like, and knows how to move toward that. It is like having a sore muscle: it "wants" to be massaged. Ruth's sore places, too, "want" something. Perhaps her pain wants simply to speak, to say those things which were not supposed to be mentioned, to make them real. She may need to identify and to name as wrong the ways in which a culture seeped in misogyny has poisoned her. Or it may be that the overwhelming powerlessness to help others in Viet Nam has become a despair of ever helping herself or anyone else. Her ability to welcome and cradle that despair may be her first experience in a long time that shows her that she can help effectively.

The fundamental criterion of feminist therapy—and, in my opinion, of all good therapy—is respect. Feminist therapy is not a technique or theory, but a stance vis-à-vis the client. It means knowing that I cannot truly know what would be forward movement for this client, though I may know how to recognize and assist it. It means that while I have much to offer the therapy process, the crucial resources lie within the person before me. It means understanding that for all my skill as a guide, I am blind, and that if I forget that fact, we are both lost.

It is my task as the therapist to be with Ruth in the way that she needs to be with herself and to guide her dialogue, with herself. If I can care about her without coddling her, if I can show her how to ask and listen to that in her which knows the way toward wholeness, then I will have the privilege of accompanying Ruth as she nurses herself toward her own health.

A Piece of the World:
Some Thoughts About Ruth

Binnie C. Klein

Ruth's story becomes all the more timely in light of our recent commemoration of the tenth anniversary of the ending of the Viet Nam war, as we struggle once again to make sense of the massive horrors that so many suffered. In the National Association of Social Work News (June 1985), the legacies of that war are examined, a war that the veterans "had long tried to forget, a war which represented the major trauma in their experience, a war that had changed their lives forever" (p. 5). The Veterans Administration reports an additional demand for counseling services that has resulted in the planned opening of 52 more facilities.

Ruth's case requires that we think in a special way, because of the profound historical events which resound in her situation. This exploration will be about an *approach,* a preliminary stance or attitude, rather than a clinical guide, as we think psychologically about the universal themes which *must* preoccupy us.

The incorporation of some Jungian theory and perspective can be of benefit in approaching Ruth's situation. As with other andocentric psychologies, we acknowledge the biases of Jung's works when they attempt to apply ideas about men's development to women. But concepts of the collective unconscious, the shadow, transformation, and individuation have more universal application. Jung offered a notion of wholeness as opposed to pathology. He chose to focus upon the psyche but felt that society and the social experience of history are ultimately the main suppliers of the individual psyche. If we agree with Jungian psychologist James Hillman's idea that psychotherapy "must take into account the sickness

Binnie C. Klein, M.S.W., is a writer and psychotherapist in New Haven, Connecticut. She is an instructor for the Connecticut Association for Jungian Psychology.

of the world" (1983, p. 136), then the nightmare of war and its effects upon a woman like Ruth must be considered as a collective dilemma. Hillman notes that in most modern psychiatric treatment patients are led to think that any problem that comes up must be because of something in them, not because of something in the world. Historically, we note this to be true of the medical and psychiatric treatment of women in particular. He insists that psychotherapy must then involve a cultivation of the imagination and a constant noticing of the world itself.

Ruth's therapist contrasts Ruth's history prior to joining the Navy with the drastic changes she was then to experience, suggesting that the Viet Nam experience was the major stressor and precipitant of her difficulties. She comes into therapy with her symptoms, yes, but also with a *piece of the world* on which her psyche is dependent. One of Ruth's primary "symptoms" is a lingering, haunting sense of *guilt,* and in her case it is not a guilt for something "bad" she has done, something immoral or unethical. It is the irrational presence of a subjective feeling of guilt. For survivors of war, there are many situations which can lead to survivors' guilt. Among them—a soldier may survive and his/her buddies do not; in order to survive, a soldier may have to engage in behavior he/she would normally find repugnant; a soldier may avoid certain life-threatening situations in which a friend gets killed; medical personnel watch people die they are unable to help. The guilt has been shown to be extremely debilitating, leading to self-destructive behavior, substance abuse, problems in relationships and work. Ruth was a nurse involved in the active combat of treating the wounded while under constant threat of harm to herself and her patients.

What is the experience of someone returning from a war without *visible* scars? We get the sense that Ruth feels inauthentic as a Viet Nam vet. Her hallucinations and dreams suggest a sense of guilt which she attempts to expiate in her cutting and suicidal behaviors. Why is Ruth feeling guilty after having served in an altruistic and unselfish role? In an issue of *Parabola* devoted to the theme of guilt, editor Lorraine Kisly says "We most often think of guilt in terms of something we have done, but this does not explain the feeling

of responsibility for an unknown something we are *not* doing"
(1983, p. 3). One aspect of Ruth's therapy could be to explore
the unknown something and give it words. Is she feeling that
while the soldiers died, she survived, that she herself was not
wounded?

As Jung said in *Essays on Contemporary Events,* "Psychological collective guilt is a *tragic fate.* It hits everybody, just
and unjust alike, everybody who was anywhere near the place
where the terrible thing happened . . . It is true that collective guilt is a most ancient and primitive *magical uncleanli-
ness"* (1947, p. 48). The histories of the world's religions are
filled with ceremonies, rituals, *things to be done* about guilt.
But what happens when there is no ritual, no model, no direction? In part, this is what has happened to Ruth and other
survivors. Jung:

> We find in fact that even the most primitive peoples take
> certain drastic measures at all those periods of life where
> psychic transitions have to be effected. . . . All these
> ceremonies . . . probably serve primarily to avert psychic
> injuries which are otherwise likely to occur at such times;
> but they are also intended to impart to the initiant the
> teaching and preparation necessary for life.

Whenever the customs fall away, "the tribe loses its soul and
is disintegrated" (p. 20–21).

Ruth "identified her Viet Nam experience as the point
from which she began to depart from her religious beliefs,
both in practice and in her ability to believe in a caring diety." For a woman with considerable religious training and
background, this represents a significant loss. And when Ruth
looks to the world around her for guidance on how to negotiate this experience, what does she find? A code of silence.
"The expectation was held by her colleagues that none of
them would discuss their feelings about working in a war
zone." In order to get through the horror it cannot be spoken
about, and alcohol becomes a significant part of the need to
alter reality and make life bearable. "The opportunity to care
for a patient until recovery did not exist." Attachments to
patients are aborted; her memories can only be of suffering,

without relief or resolution. The safety of her world and her person diminishes, as she encounters death both at work and while off duty. The boundaries blur, and she begins to feel more and more fragile. Under such circumstances, so many of us would. And yet, Ruth accuses herself of fabricating her symptoms and wonders if her symptoms are real. When Ruth returns to the U.S. the collective denial continues. Her somatic symptoms are misdiagnosed, and she is given a long, nine month stay in a neuropsychiatric hospital. The message is "you're crazy." Her psychiatrist prescribes a tranquilizer and *actively* discourages her from discussing the Viet Nam experience. The message is "it's not real . . . be silent." It is difficult to comtemplate this aspect of her experience without feeling a sense of outrage and sadness.

Two ideas informed by Jungian concepts will be helpful here. (1) The idea of a symptom as a "degraded" *symbol;* and (2) The only suffering which we cannot endure is that which has no meaning.

A symbol represents something, pointing beyond itself to a meaning not conveyed by a rational term. It is, in a way, the best expression possible of something somewhat mysterious. When I use the term "degraded" I mean something which has been lowered in estimation, brought into contempt. Think of Moses, the prophets, hearing voices, having hallucinations, primitive people experiencing the "shock" of voices, panics, etc., which they would feel were caused by spirits or gods. We call these events "symptoms," "pathological," and are naturally very frightened by them when they happen to us. And we don't have much of a social or cultural context in which to place these events; instead we privately and individually join the legion of people using psychotherapy for individual journeys of self-discovery. A symptom is *an indication of something;* the unconscious expresses conflict through production of symptoms. If we can view Ruth's symptoms as symbolic experiences, we can ask what the symbols are, and what they seem to want from her. She has hallucinations of the dead and maimed bodies; she smells them. Sounds trigger memories of sudden evacuations. To relieve anxiety and pressure she cuts herself, and only then can cry, or sleep.

In effect, she is re-experiencing the terror of her Viet Nam experience, attempting to serve two goals: (1) to punish herself for the subjective experience of guilt; and (2) to make sense of the horror. Her therapist states that one of her goals of therapy is to "come to terms with the overt and symbolic meanings of her life experiences since her service in the Navy began." The symbolic experience is then one of a repetitive *ritual* in which Ruth is in effect "back" in Viet Nam. An obsession is an attempt to get to meaning, to work something until we can let go of it. These experiences intrude upon her everyday living, making her life a living hell, as Viet Nam was a living hell. She begins to isolate herself, numbing her emotional responses, a process that was essential for survival under war conditions. Emotions of grieving had to be put on hold, and now, in the expression of these experiences, Ruth struggles to play out the unresolved conflicts and feelings. Her psyche becomes, in effect, a "battleground." The hope embodied in the guilt is for the transformation of unresolved conflict into reconciliation. In primitive societies, in the history of other wars of Western civilization, that process was aided by collective rituals. As ex-Army nurse Lynda Van Devanter notes in *Home Before Morning,* an account of her own experience in Viet Nam,

> When the soldiers of World War II came home, they were met by brass bands, ticker-tape parades, and people so thankful for their service that even those who had never heard a shot fired in anger were treated with respect. It was a time when words like honor, glory, and duty held some value, a time when a returning GI was viewed with esteem so high it bordered on awe. . . . If you had answered your country's call, you were a hero. And in those days, heroes were plentiful. (1983, p. 245)

Yet the circumstances of the Viet Nam War allowed no positive or healing ritual for the return of the heroes and their integration back into civilian life. We are only just beginning to hear of the range of the Veterans' experience as they have attempted to get back into the mainstream, often with disastrous results. Even with the more "normal" return of Veterans from World War II, the Veterans' hospitals were filled with men and women suffering from the after-effects of their experience. Can we speak of *any* warfare as a tolerable stress?

Jung felt that when a disorder or chaos breaks into our order of things we really need a regular *rite de sortie:* a sort of ceremony to deal with the guilt, both real and imagined. The archetypal image of the soldier/hero/nurse involved in war-time is that of individuality subsumed to the will of the collective. But in our modern times, rites of transformation have turned inward, for the individual person to resolve.

Ruth's recurrent nightmare of being "sought out and hurt by badly wounded men she had cared for in Da Nang and New York" can be seen as the story her psyche creates. Unlike the Freudian view that the dream disguises its content so as not to shock the dreamer into waking, Jung felt that there was no reason to assume that the dream was a crafty device trying to lead us astray. He saw the dream as a normal, spontaneous, and creative expression of the unconscious, a story with a beginning, a middle, and an end. In this system of dream analysis, one stays close to the specific details and symbols of the dream itself, paying more attention to the form and content of the dream than to the free associations of the dreamer. And yet, with the method of *amplification,* one can extend the significance of a particular dream image when possible with elements taken from mythological and ethnological parallels.

Ruth's dream image is one of pursuit. A paraphrase of the dream might be:

> I am being pursued, hunted by those who are trained to hunt. I am found (I am revealed to be guilty). But these men are not whole, they are wounded. I know them. I have seen them before. I had tried to help them once (I couldn't save them). They are furious with me for not saving them. I am furious with myself for not saving them. I am furious with myself for having survived when they did not. I need to punish myself—I have them do it for me.

The story Ruth's dream tells is one of an imagined crime and punishment. The wounded men could also be seen as personifications of the *shadow,* the devalued and despised parts of the Self which one attempts to push down into the unconscious. Ruth herself has been psychologically wounded by the War, yet she never seems to feel that her wounds are real. Only the visible, tangible wounds of the physically maimed represent valid hurts to her.

Van Devanter was plagued by a similar dream:

> Pseudomonas (common infection of burn victims) was everywhere. Soldiers and Vietnamese ran into the OR with napalm oozing down their backs carrying flames with it as they screamed in agony. They pressed against me, smothering me with burned and decaying flesh until I was scratching at them, tearing away hunks of meat so I could get some fresh air. *But they wouldn't let me go.* (p. 330) [emphasis mine]

In other nightmares, she is visited by severely wounded men she treated who haunt her with one question: "Why?"

That is the echo of the irreconcilable anguish—suffering without meaning. The despair and depression come with the experience of senselessness. Our human inclination is to fashion meaning; we are storytellers. Looking up at the Moon and Sun, our ancestors told stories of their creation and soothed their own fear and questioning. Violence in nature was explained by "emotions" of the Gods.

Ruth and the other Veterans will not invent a comforting story. Some questions will always remain unanswered. But perhaps the *process* of seeking meaning and understanding is a vital element. There are different kinds of knowledge—one kind comes through the mind, like a bird; another rises up from deep within, like a fish, from what one has experienced through suffering.

Individuation is the gradual realization of the Self over a lifetime; the achievement of a personal blend between the collective and universal and what is unique and individual. It is a process, not a state, a movement towards wholeness which implies a recognition and acceptance of parts of the Self that may seem negative or are repugnant. The symbolism of birth, life, death and rebirth is part of the pattern of the individuation process.

The individual experience of the symbolic death and rebirth

often comes through struggle and suffering. Ruth could not have anticipated the journey she would undertake by joining the military and asking to serve in Viet Nam. In mythological terms, its corollary would be a "descent into hell"—a symbolic death. She undergoes a radical psychic upheaval that requires a new attitude in her conscious life, an attitude she will work on in her therapy. In the individuation process the "missing" element is always being sought and integrated. Unfortunately, the collective response and model for this process in regard to the Viet Nam War is sorely incomplete. Patti Coleen Brown (1984) notes that "as a society we have not yet adequately brought closure to the Viet Nam experience." In part this would involve allowing "nonjudgmentally and openly for the veteran's catharsis about the character and meaning of his/her involvements and perspectives of the war past and present" (p. 378). For Ruth one of the key elements of her process will be an acceptance of the life experiences she has had and all of the ways she has coped with them.

REFERENCES

Brown, P.C. (1984). Legacies of a war: treatment considerations with Vietnam veterans and their families. *Social Work, 29,* 372–380.
Hillman, J. (1983). *Inter Views.* New York: Harper and Row.
Jung, C.G. (1947). *Essays on Contemporary Events.* London: Kegan Paul.
Kisly, L. (1983). Focus. *Parabola, 8,* 2–3.
National Association for Social Work News (June 1985), 5–6.
Van Devanter, Lynda. (1984). *Home Before Morning.* New York: Warner Books.

Re-Evaluation Counseling: A Self-Help Model for Recovery From Emotional Distress

Phyllis Bronstein

I was invited to discuss this case from the perspective of family therapy, which is my main area of academic teaching and clinical supervision. However, after reading the case description, I found it very difficult to conceptualize the client's problem from that perspective. Most approaches to family therapy, whether they are labeled structural, strategic, systemic, or eclectic, view the family as a *system* with a life of its own, and the symptomatic behavior of a particular family member as a function of that system (e.g., Minuchin, 1974; Madanes, 1984; Weeks & L'Abate, 1982; Hoffman, 1981; Papp, 1983). The family is seen as keeping itself mobilized around the symptomatic behavior (which it unconsciously works to perpetuate), in order to avoid dealing with more frightening problems or feelings. Thus it is able to stay together, often in an overly-involved or "enmeshed" way, without risking change or dissolution. The symptomatic behavior is maintained by the system as a means the family has come up with to keep going—without going anywhere.

In considering the case of Ruth, it seemed very unlikely that her intense emotional distress, her self-mutilative behavior, and her alcoholism were being maintained as part of an ongoing family system. In fact, the case history indicates that she had withdrawn socially and emotionally from all family members except her youngest sister. While *early* family relationships, as described in the case history, might have affected

---

Phyllis Bronstein received her Ph.D. at Harvard, held a clinical post-doctoral fellowship in Ethnicity and Mental Health at the Harvard Medical School, taught at Wellesley College, and is currently on the clinical faculty at the University of Vermont. Her research has been in the areas of family and group interaction, parent-child relations, gender role socialization, and women's professional advancement.

her personality development and the course her later life took, family systems therapy focuses primarily on family interactions and relationships in the present, and these apparently were not salient for Ruth. Given that fact, it seemed more useful to consider her family dynamics in terms of how early family structure and relationships might have shaped her personality and her responses to later life situations—and to view her more appropriately as a candidate for individual treatment.

EARLY FAMILY DYNAMICS:
EFFECTS ON LATER FUNCTIONING

Looking over the background information in order to plan an effective treatment approach, I was struck by the ways in which some of the details of Ruth's childhood seemed consistent with the details of her later years, in terms of the kinds of life choices she made, and the means she developed for coping with emotional distress. Within her family, as the eldest (and model) daughter, and "junior mother" to her disabled sister, she was reinforced for being responsible and independent, in particular, for taking care of others, and for not requiring that others take care of her. Unable to get attention from her parents, she gave up trying, and withdrew into comforts (such as solitude and reading) that she could provide for herself. As a result of this family dynamic, it appears that she came to believe that her only value to others, and her only way to connect with them, was in being a caretaker—and that she would also have to be the one to take care of herself. In addition, she apparently came to believe that painful emotion could not be expressed to others, and that it was better, if possible, not to feel it at all. Thus it is not surprising that she chose nursing as her profession, and that later, when suffering from severe emotional distress, she was unable to make use of social support from family, old friends, and therapeutic groups, but instead sought solace in the numbing effects of alcohol.

In addition, her devout Catholic background and parochial school education very likely left Ruth with a deep-rooted belief in her own sinfulness (McGoldrick, 1982; Langelier,

1982). This is suggested by her strong (probably compensatory) drive to be "good," a tendency to accept (or self-inflict) punishment for "sinful" feelings as well as behavior, and an apparent belief that her suffering was both deserved and ennobling. Thus her becoming a Navy nurse during the time of the Viet Nam War may have provided a potent combination of goodness, self-sacrifice, and suffering, while her "sinful" liason with a married man brought sexual and emotional abuse, which she accepted over a substantial period of time. Further, her "selfish" longings for attention and help when she was in desperate emotional straits were countered with extreme self-accusatory behavior, and her intense anxiety at that time was relieved only by self-mutilation.

Up until her Navy experiences, Ruth appeared to have been functioning very well. However, nothing in her earlier years had prepared her for what she was to encounter, and the coping mechanisms she had developed in those years were insufficient to handle such a prolonged and intensely stressful life situation. Her main mechanism for feeling valuable to and connected with others—the caretaker role that so many women assume (Miller, 1976)—became traumatic and demoralizing. On the one hand, she was exposed daily to the threat of military attack, and to badly maimed, dying, and dead human beings. On the other, since the wounded stayed in the hospital until they either died or were sufficiently stabilized to be evacuated, she was not able to feel the rewards of being an effective caretaker, as she did not get to see her efforts result in their recovery. In addition, as in her earlier family situation, she was unable to get the kind of attention and caretaking that she needed from others. Her colleagues were not open to sharing feelings about their experiences, and her lover was abusive. Further, on returning to the States, her serious physical condition was misdiagnosed as psychosomatic, which resulted in a nine-month inappropriate and harmful stay in a neuropsychiatric hospital, and four years of therapy with an at best incompetent psychiatrist. These experiences could only have served to confirm her early-formed belief that no one would ever really take care of her, and that she could count only on herself for comfort. Moreover, the fact that neither her colleagues in Viet Nam nor the psychiatrist afterwards would allow her to express her feelings about the horrors she had encountered, and the fact that the psychiatrist kept her on Valium for four years, must have further reinforced her belief that it would be inappropriate, and perhaps dangerous, to let herself fully experience those feelings. Thus it is not surprising that she fell back on taking care of herself, withdrawing from social and therapeutic contact, and making increasing use of alcohol to suppress the feelings that threatened to overwhelm her. And it is not surprising, given the intense and extended emotional (and physical) traumas she had undergone, that alcohol eventually was not enough.

MOVING TOWARD RECOVERY

Therapeutic Priorities and Goals

In considering what would be an appropriate treatment plan, I came up with several interrelated priorities and goals, which are slightly different from (but overlap with) the goals Ruth herself set up. My first priority would be to try to contradict her sense of isolation, so that she would begin to see that she is not permanently and totally alone in her distress, and that someone can and will help her. Toward this end, I would have her come in initially for three therapy sessions a week. In addition I would encourage her to continue in her AA and VA therapeutic groups, in hopes that she would eventually be able to begin forming relationships within them, and utilizing the support that they offer. My next priority would be to provide a safe place, within those sessions, for her to allow herself to feel—and release—the intensely painful emotions she had been trying to suppress for so many years. Initially, the focus would certainly be on her war experiences, since they are the source of her most powerful and distressing symptoms. In addition, she might at some point re-examine the painful aftermath of those years, including her illness and hospitalization. Eventually, she would come to address earlier issues from her family history, and begin to allow herself to feel and release long-suppressed feelings of longing, sadness, guilt, and anger. A main goal of the therapy would be for Ruth to develop a strong sense of her own worth—for her to realize that she is and has always been a perfectly fine and valuable person. This would necessitate her relinquishing the long-held beliefs that she must demonstrate her goodness and her usefulness in order to earn a place in the world, and that she deserves to suffer. A final goal would be for her to establish ongoing social support, which would ideally include becoming part of a self-help growth and support network such as the one described below. These priorities and goals would, I believe, allow her to achieve not only the goals she set for herself, but also to acquire a means for continuing to recover from any damage retained from the past, and to develop her fullest potential for emotional well-being and effective functioning in the world.

Therapeutic Approach: Re-Evaluation Counseling

Background and theory. The therapeutic approach that I feel would most effectively lead to Ruth's recovery is Re-Evaluation Counseling (Jackins, 1970, 1973, 1977, 1978, 1981, 1983). Re-Evaluation Counseling is both a comprehensive theory of personality and human functioning, and a counseling method that can be used in individual, couple, or group situations. It has three basic premises:

1. that human beings have enormous potential for intelligence, creativity, love, cooperation, and zestful enjoyment of life;
2. that the emotional and physical hurts people experience, and the painful emotions they are left with as a result, diminish functioning and interfere with the realization of that potential—and that the effects of those hurts are cumulative over time;
3. that it is possible to completely recover the enormous potential that humans have through a process of releasing or discharging the accumulated painful emotion.

Re-Evaluation Counseling theory maintains that the full and open expression of emotion, or emotional discharge as it will hereafter be called, is a natural healing process which enables individuals to recover from a present or past distress-

ing event or condition. It is to be distinguished from emotional *arousal* or *distress,* a tension state with various physiological components, including autonomic nervous system
arousal, which occurs in response to the distressing event or
condition. Emotional discharge is the spontaneous *release* of
that tension through involuntary bodily processes such as crying, trembling, angry outburst, laughter, and sweating.[1] It is
an essential part of the psychological recovery process from
the distressing situation, by means of letting go of the painful
feelings (along with the physiological tensions) that have been
aroused. According to Re-Evaluation Counseling theory, if
those feelings are not released, they interfere with individuals'
ability to process the distressing event in a way that allows
them to fully understand, recover, and learn from the experience. Instead, a rigid and automatic pattern of response develops in the area of the distress, as an attempt to cope with
the situation and avoid feeling the painful emotions—and this
rigid pattern tends to replay itself, like a recording, whenever
something reminiscent of the original distress experience occurs. In this way, the potential humans have for rational,
loving, creative, and zestful behavior is increasingly limited
and obscured by cumulative distress.

Common phrases such as "a good laugh," "a good cry," and
"getting it off one's chest," attest to our awareness of the
beneficial nature of the emotional discharge process. Yet
awareness does not translate easily into every day interactions
with friends and family, nor even into interactions between
therapist and client. Usually, that natural healing process is not
allowed to proceed. Most people ascribe to cultural values and
norms that disparage and discourage emotional discharge
(which include behavioral labels such as "self-pitying," "hysterical," and "out of control," and character attributions such
as "weak," "dependent," "helpless," and "childish"). In addition, people mistakenly tend to equate emotional discharge
with the hurt itself, instead of seeing it as the *un*-hurting process. They treat it like a symptom of physical illness; if they can
remove the symptom, the illness will be cured—and if they can
stop the crying (or trembling, or raging), the emotional distress
will vanish. A further likelihood is that a person's emotional
discharge may come uncomfortably close to triggering list-
eners' awareness and discharge of their own long-repressed

painful emotions, so that they will generally move quickly to prevent or curtail the process. Thus, with distressed babies, we pat and jiggle and feed and rock and distract with funny faces and toys. With older children we add various forms of reassurance, persuasion, and shame ("There, there, that didn't really hurt," "Stop acting like a baby").[2] With adults, we add analyzing, rationalizing, and intellectualizing—as we help the person *discuss* the painful emotion instead of feeling it. This is true for many therapists, who may at first welcome a show of feelings as evidence that an important issue is being addressed, but who then persist in addressing the issue, rather than allowing the painful feelings to discharge fully.

The notion that emotional discharge has healing or cleansing properties of course did not originate with Re-Evaluation Counseling. It goes back more than 2000 years, to Aristotle's *Poetics* (1968), which presents the idea that people's strong emotional reactions to stage tragedies serve to purge them of pity and terror. In addition, emotional discharge has frequently been found to be a major element in the healing rituals of primitive cultures throughout the world (Nichols & Zax, 1977; Scheff, 1979). The healing effect of emotional discharge was also an essential component in the early formulations of modern psychotherapy; Freud and Breuer (1966) proposed that the cure of hysterical symptoms could be achieved by the client's re-experiencing an early traumatic experience (abreaction), and discharging the repressed painful emotions surrounding that experience (catharsis). This particular therapeutic approach, using hypnosis (as Freud and Breuer had done) or drugs to facilitate abreaction, was used extensively for the treatment of psychological casualties from both World Wars; soldiers were helped to re-experience traumatic battle experiences, and release undischarged terror, rage, and grief that had resulted from them (Nichols & Zax, 1977). However, Freud early on began to move toward a much more cognitive approach, focusing on the history and meaning of neurotic symptoms rather than on symptom relief through catharsis. This change affected the overall direction of psychoanalytic therapy, so that catharsis came to be regarded as more of a supplementary therapeutic event than the main curative factor. Expressive methods of psychotherapy did develop outside the psychoanalytic mainstream, reaching a peak of popularity during the Human Potential Movement of the 1960s and early 1970s, though more recent psychotherapeutic trends have been in the direction of cognitive, behavioral, and systemic approaches.

Perhaps it is because of the continued non-mainstream status of expressive therapies that very little systematic research has been conducted to measure their efficacy. However, what little research there is strongly supports the positive effects of emotional discharge. A study by Nichols (1974) found that patients who showed the highest levels of emotional discharge improved significantly more on behavioral goals and showed greater improvement on a measure of satisfaction with their lives than those with low levels of discharge. Karle, Corriere, & Hart (1973) found that patients in primal therapy, a highly cathartic method, showed a significant decrease in indicators of bodily tension such as pulse, blood pressure, and temperature, though whether the changes resulted from emotional discharge or other therapeutic factors was not clear. Nichols and Zax (1977), reviewing studies of implosive therapy, which is grounded in behavioral principles but often generates strong emotional discharge, found overall that patients treated with this method improved significantly more than patients treated with traditional methods. Implosive therapy has recently proved to be helpful with Viet Nam veterans suffering from posttraumatic stress disorders (Fairbank & Keane, 1982; Keane & Kaloupek, 1982), whereas a stress management approach has proved to be less effective, with a much higher drop-out rate (Keane, personal communication). And Yalom (1975), in a study asking therapy group patients to rank order the curative factors of their own therapy, found that catharsis was ranked second in a list of twelve general categories that emerged.

In addition, data are becoming available on the negative effects of *not* releasing emotions. Crepeau (1980) found that people suffering from ulcers and colitis had a significantly more negative attitude toward crying, and reported crying far less often than healthy controls. Similarly, Schwartz (1983) found that people reporting "impoverished blends of emotions" had more physical illnesses. And current research on the personality dynamics of people found to have cancer suggests that suppression of emotion may play a contributory role in the development and course of the disease (Levy, 1983; Associated Press, 1983; Kneier & Temoshok, 1984).

The Practice of Re-Evaluation Counseling

Re-Evaluation Counseling (RC) exists as a world-wide self-help growth movement, loosely organized into small communities and larger areas, all of which connect back to a central office in Seattle. The founder, main theorist, and central leader is Harvey Jackins, who has written numerous articles and books on the subject, and who conducts frequent workshops and conferences within the world-wide community. The counseling process (which is also called "co-counseling") is done exclusively on a peer-to-peer reciprocal basis, with no money exchanged between co-counselors; instead, during a session, co-counselors exchange time by alternating turns being counselor and client. Certified RC teachers, on the other hand, do receive remuneration for the classes and workshops they lead. RC communities, depending on their size and particular interests, may offer co-counselor training classes at beginning and advanced levels, and a range of workshops and support groups focusing on specific populations or issues. The overall RC movement has a strong commitment to human liberation, with designated leaders within the world RC community who focus their energies on liberation issues for specific populations. In addition, there are approximately thirty journals produced by special interest groups within the worldwide community, most of which focus on liberation issues (e.g., *Black Re-Emergence, Our Asian Inheritance, Sisters, Wide World Changing*).

Although most people who learn and use RC are not mental health professionals, the mental health professionals who learn it frequently incorporate the theory and technique into the therapeutic work they do. However, since their counseling is non-reciprocal, since they receive a fee for their services, and since they may be blending RC theory and technique with other methods they do not label or advertise what they do as Re-Evaluation Counseling; the name is reserved for the approved and regulated practices that go on within the worldwide RC community. Membership in RC community classes is limited to those who are currently functioning well enough to be able to serve as effective co-counselors for others. Thus were Ruth to apply to join a co-counseling class, she would most probably be urged to seek one-way counseling or therapy first, and to re-apply at such time when she would have sufficient attention outside of her own distress to be able to give it effectively in a co-counseling relationship. If she were to come to me at this point for individual treatment, I would use my training in Re-Evaluation Counseling as a basis for the work I would do with her. Ultimately, when she would have reached the point of readiness, I would hope to steer her toward learning co-counseling skills, and becoming part of the RC self-help support network.

Working With Ruth

My primary task with Ruth would be to provide the safety she would need to re-experience and release the painful emotions she has been trying to suppress for so long. This would be accomplished through several means. First, of course, I would listen—attentively, permissively, and caringly. Second, I would communicate to her my belief in the healing properties of emotional discharge, thereby making it an instrument of hope and cure, rather than a symptom of her psychopathology, and giving her permission to let it happen. Third, in my interactions with her and in my demeanor, I would communicate and model hopefulness and confidence—in my ability to help her, in her full recovery, and in the essentially benign nature of the world. Finally, in my working to facilitate her emotional discharge, I would strive to provide what RC calls a "contradiction of the distress." RC theory proposes that discharge will occur spontaneously if the client's distressed feelings can be sufficiently contradicted by some element of hope or safety. If this contradiction does not occur, the client will remain caught up in the rigid response pattern that developed as a way of coping with the original distress, and in the sanctions against discharge that were operative at that time. In that case, the painful emotions will very likely remain inaccessible, and the client may seem to be numb, or to have "shut down" emotionally. One basic way for the counselor or therapist to contradict the distress, and thereby promote discharge, is to continually remind the client of her presence as a safe, supportive other. Thus, for example, if Ruth had been crying, but then lapsed into staring at her lap and talking in a monotone, I would conclude that she was becoming overwhelmed by past distress, and would try to connect with her. I might try to get her to make eye contact, by simply saying, "Hi, Ruth," or I might touch her arm, or take her hand, to let her feel my presence. If her feelings were still too overwhelming, I might move in close and hold her, so that she could more fully be aware of my being there with her in present time reality. Or I might ask her to repeat a phrase that directly contradicted the heaviness of the terror, or the grief—something optimistic, or absurd, or outrageous, such as "It's a beautiful world out there," or "Their mothers should've taught them to look both ways when crossing a mine field." If the phrase were an effective contradiction, she would probably never manage to say it, but would simply keep discharging as I cheerfully repeated it. Incidentally, of the two examples provided, the first would be likely to evoke tears and/or trembling, while the second would probably evoke laughter, which might at some point change to tears or trembling. On the other hand, if Ruth were avoiding dealing with her past distress by focusing only on present day problems, I would probably ask her to tell me what one of those problems reminded her of, or the times she had had similar problems or feelings in the past—or I might simply keep encouraging her to tell me about the terrible things she had been through. And as she began to focus on the distress experiences of the past, I would be ready to provide the kind of contradiction described above, letting her know that it was finally a safe time and place for her to feel— and express—her feelings.

My second task in working with Ruth would be to help her recover her self-esteem. Re-Evaluation Counseling theory holds that distressful experiences generally involve the instilling of negative feelings about the self, and that recovery from the distress can be facilitated by directly contradicting those feelings—i.e., by the client's attempting to completely appreciate herself in all areas. The counselor helps in this process in two ways: (1) by directly complimenting the client, letting her know how capable, lovable, and valuable she is, and (2) by directing the client to make positive statements about

herself, and about how she should be regarded and treated by
others. Such compliments or statements, if they accurately
contradict the negativity and despair of the past, will allow
emotional discharge to occur. Sufficient discharge of painful
emotion will then be followed by a *re-evaluation* of the distress
experience in the light of present reality, and an exchanging of
the rigid pattern of feelings and behaviors that developed from
it for a positive, rational outlook and self-concept. In working
with Ruth, I would want to contradict her feelings of being
valued only for her caretaker role, and of not meriting attention from others. Thus I might direct her to say, in a confident
voice, that she is worthy of great love, or that she deserves
everyone's undivided attention—or I might direct her to stand
up and say confidently and delightedly, "Here I am," imagin-
ing herself walking into a room full of people. We might also
focus on distress instilled by her Catholic upbringing, which
would probably involve her attempting to affirm her inherent
goodness, and make confident statements about all the plea-
sures she deserves in life. Of course, the above are merely a
sampling of possible interventions using a Re-Evaluation
Counseling approach. A myriad of other possibilities exist,
depending both on the material the client presents (both verbally and non-verbally) during the session, and on the sensitiv-
ity and ingenuity of the counselor or therapist.

Ongoing Self-Help: The Re-Evaluation Counseling Community

The final stage of "therapy" that I would recommend for
Ruth would be an ongoing one. I see her as becoming a
skilled co-counselor within a Re-Evaluation Counseling Community, which would provide her with the support and mechanisms she would need to continue her re-emergence from
past distress, and her increasingly positive functioning in the
world. She might, in addition to participating in an RC class
and co-counseling sessions, join an RC support group. A
women's group, for example, might provide Ruth with support from women like herself, who were striving to move
beyond the caretaker role in empowering themselves in the
world. Or she might join a group of co-counselors who were
raised Catholic, and wanted to share experiences and discharge their distress in that area. At this time, Ruth would

also be moving ahead in the career direction she would have by then chosen, and would be building and re-building relationships with friends and family. I see her emerging as a knowledgeable and powerful woman, deepened but no longer damaged by her experiences, and able to receive caring and support from others without feeling obligated to take care of them. I would not be surprised to see her assume a position of leadership—perhaps within the RC community, perhaps among Viet Nam veterans, perhaps in the peace movement. Once Ruth would have recovered from the distresses of the past, there would be no limits in realizing her potential.

NOTES

1. More detailed descriptions of this process can be found in Jackins (1970, 1978) and Scheff (1979).
2. An analysis of emotional discharge from a developmental/socialization perspective can be found in Bronstein, 1984. Some of the following discussion of history and research is taken from that article.

REFERENCES

Aristotle (1968). *Poetics*. D.W. Lucas (Ed.), Oxford, England: Clarendon Press.
Associated Press (1983). Scientists on the track of the cancer-prone personality. *Burlington (VT) Free Press,* January 25.
Bronstein, P. (1984). Promoting healthy emotional development in children. *Journal of Primary Prevention, 5* (2), Winter, 92–110.
Crepeau, M. T. (1982). A comparison of the behavior patterns and meanings of weeping among adult men and women across three health conditions. Paper presented at the annual meeting of the American Psychological Association, Washington, D.C.
Fairbank, J. A. & Keane, T. M. (1982). Flooding for combat-related stress disorders: Assessment of anxiety reduction across traumatic memories. *Behavior Therapy, 13,* 499–510.
Freud, S. & Breuer, J. (1966). *Studies on hysteria* (1895). New York: Avon Books.
Hoffman, L. (1981). *Foundations of family therapy*. New York: Basic Books.
Jackins, H. (1970). *Fundamentals of co-counseling manual*. Seattle: Rational Island Publishers.
Jackins, H. (1973). *The human situation*. Seattle: Rational Island Publishers.
Jackins, H. (1975). *Guidebook to re-evaluation counseling*. Seattle: Rational Island Publishers.
Jackins, H. (1977). *The upward trend*. Seattle: Rational Island Publishers.
Jackins, H. (1978). *The human side of human beings*. Seattle: Rational Island Publishers.
Jackins, H. (1981). *The benign reality*. Seattle: Rational Island Publishers.
Jackins, H. (1983). *The reclaiming of power*. Seattle: Rational Island Publishers.

Karle, W., Corriere, R., & Hart, J. (1973). Psychophysiological changes in abreactive therapy: Study 1, primal therapy. *Psychotherapy: Theory, Research, and Practice, 10* (2), Summer, 117–122.

Keane, T. M., & Kaloupek, D. G. (1982). Imaginal flooding in the treatment of posttraumatic stress disorder. *Journal of Consulting and Clinical Psychology, 50,* 138–140.

Kneier, A. & Temoshok, L. (1984). Repressive coping reactions in patients with malignant melanoma as compared to cardiovascular disease patients. *Journal of Psychosomatic Research, 28* (2), 145–155.

Langelier, R. (1982). French Canadian families. In M. McGoldrick, J. K. Pearce, and J. Giordano (Eds.), *Ethnicity and family therapy.* New York: Guilford Press.

Levy, S. M. (1983). Host differences in neoplastic risk: Behavioral and social contributors to disease. *Health Psychology, 2* (1), 21–44.

Madanes, C. (1981). *Strategic family therapy.* San Francisco: Jossey-Bass.

McGoldrick, M. (1982). Irish families. In M. McGoldrick, J. K. Pearce, & J. Giordano, *Ethnicity and family therapy.* New York: Guilford Press.

Minuchin, S. (1974). *Families and family therapy.* Cambridge, MA: Harvard University Press.

Nichols, M. P. (1974). Outcome of brief cathartic psychotherapy. *Journal of Consulting and Clinical Psychology, 42,* 403–410.

Nichols, M. P. & Zax, M. (1977). *Catharsis in psychotherapy.* New York: Gardner Press.

Papp, P. (1983). *The process of change.* New York: Guilford Press.

Scheff, T. J. (1979). *Catharsis in ritual, healing, and drama.* Berkeley: University of California Press.

Schwartz, G. (1983). Psychophysiology of facial expression and emotion. Abstract submitted to the Anaheim Conference on Emotion, 1983.

Weeks, G. R. & L'Abate, L. (1982). *Paradoxical psychotherapy.* New York: Brunner/Mazel.

Yalom, I. (1975). *The theory and practice of group psychotherapy.* New York: Basic Books.

Post-Traumatic Stress Disorder in a Vietnam Nurse: Behavioral Analysis of a Case Study

Patricia A. Resick

FIRST IMPRESSIONS

Frankly, my first thought as I read Ruth's case story was that I would be thrilled to receive such extensive information on a client prior to a first session. In my work with trauma victims I have found that women are frequently initially reticent to disclose the extent of their reactions to the traumatic event. They are sometimes afraid that they are going crazy when they experience sudden mood swings, flashbacks and panic attacks, seemingly at random. They also suspect that they are coping particularly poorly because they continue to have symptoms months (or years) after the event.

While clients often go to therapists because they are afraid they are going crazy, simultaneously they may be reluctant to discuss this with the therapist for fear of having their self-diagnosis confirmed. Therefore, they may withhold information they consider particularly damning. I usually attempt to counter this tendency by making some type of normalizing statement prior to asking about suspected symptoms (e.g., "Women who have experienced this type of trauma sometimes have flashbacks and panic attacks for a long time after the incident. Have you had any problems with flashbacks or sudden fear reactions?")

Patricia A. Resick is an Associate Professor of Psychology at the University of Missouri-St. Louis, 8001 Natural Bridge Rd., St. Louis, MO 63121. She earned her doctorate at the University of Georgia and currently serves on the editorial boards of *Women & Therapy* and *Behavior Modification*. This article was written while the author was sponsored by a grant from the National Institute of Mental Health RO1 MH37296 "Reactions of Female and Male Victims of Rape or Robbery".

I had a number of other thoughts and reactions as I read the case material for the first time. We are becoming more sensitive to the trauma experienced by victims, but often continue to ignore the trauma of secondary victims. Secondary victims are those who are not directly attacked or injured, but who are traumatized by witnessing horrifying events or are the loved one of a victim. While Ruth could be considered a primary victim in that the hospital was shelled frequently, she was not injured by these attacks. It would be easy for people to overlook the trauma of her secondary victimization, the witnessing of mutilation and death. I was struck by the sheer amount of death and mutilation she witnessed paired with the stress of the constant possibility that she could be injured or killed while on or off duty.

I think there is also a societal assumption that medical personnel are unaffected by what they witness, by death and mutilation. Because injury and death are part of medical practice, we assume that caregivers become accustomed to it and are immune to trauma reactions. Perhaps that assumption also permeates the medical profession, as evidenced by the expectation of Ruth's colleagues that their feelings should not be discussed. However, their frequent use of alcohol indicates that they were indeed affected and in need of a coping strategy.

The chosen coping strategies, alcohol and silence, also struck me as particularly male strategies. Ruth was immersed in the male-dominated worlds of war and medicine. Her role models for coping were men. In reading this case material, it occurred to me how similar her symptoms were to the Viet Nam combat veterans and how difficult it would be for most women to relate to her experiences. Women are frequently excluded from or choose not to engage in discussions of Viet Nam experiences. It would have been very difficult for Ruth to find anyone to talk to even if she had wanted to.

My strongest reaction, however, was to Ruth's complete isolation. Her lack of connectedness appears somewhat confusing given her apparent popularity in adolescence. While there are certainly indications that she had developed withdrawal as a coping strategy, she did have a good level of adjustment to all appearances prior to her Viet Nam experiences. As I read that section of the case study I thought about the superficiality of most adolescent friendships and how the support of others tends to drop away following traumatic events. Being popular, intelligent and a leader does not ensure ongoing social support following major life crises. It is not unusual for family and friends to become puzzled and impatient with the intensity of reactions and lack of recovery they witness in victims of trauma. They soon conclude that the victim's reaction and inability to forget and put it behind reflects some personal weakness or failure on the part of the victim. At a time when Ruth needed tremendous social support, others probably pulled back and Ruth withdrew instead of reaching out. How lonely her life must have been. How desperate Ruth must have felt having to deal with so much terror and stress all alone. It is certainly understandable why she medicated herself with alcohol and, in overwhelming moments, used pain in the present to stop the terror from her past. Suicide would appear to be a logical option and death a place of calm and permanent relief.

CASE FORMULATION

Ruth was subjected to a constant threat of death and witnessed horrifying mutilation and death over an extended period of time. It was so constant that even when she was away from work and thought she could relax (having lunch with a friend) she encountered it. In my work with rape and robbery victims, I have found that a single incidence of life-threatening violence is sufficient to classically condition fear reactions (e.g., flashbacks, panic attacks) to stimuli that were present in the assault situation. Understandably, the conditioned fear reactions are so unpleasant that victims frequently escape from and then avoid stimuli that remind them of the event.

The escape and avoidance serve to maintain the conditioned fear reactions, and over time phobias develop. Those stimuli that are not avoided eventually extinguish as danger signals. Occasionally, stimuli are not actively avoided but are of low frequency in the normal environment so they don't extinguish either. In Ruth's case, helicopters and explosions are low frequency events that continue to trigger terror reactions. Stimuli can be visual, auditory, tactile, olfactory, temporal or cognitive. What were referred to as visual and olfactory hallucinations in this case study are, most probably, intense flashbacks induced by environmental stimuli or cognitions. Ruth may well have used alcohol, at least partially, to suppress cognitions that triggered flashbacks as well as to suppress the flashbacks and fear reactions themselves.

In addition to conditioned reactions, trauma victims, such as violent crime victims, are influenced by a variety of cognitive mediators. Prior to victimization, people hold attributions regarding the likelihood of being victimized, who gets victimized and why, and how they would or would not cope with trauma. Such attributions can augment or impede coping efforts and affect self-esteem. Self-esteem can drop when prior expectations about coping are not met.

Attributions about the world, as well as the self, are likely to change following trauma. When trauma-conditioned stimuli continue to trigger terror reactions that feel similar to the actual event, the victim naturally begins to feel that the world is a very dangerous place even when, in reality, it is not. Feeling safe in a rather dangerous world may be accomplished partly by developing certain attributions about who gets victimized. The "just world" belief is that good things happen to good people and bad things happen to bad people. Many religions reinforce this belief. When people believe in a just world they feel safe because they assume that bad things won't happen to them as long as they behave correctly and are good people. After facing such an onslaught of senseless violence and suffering, it is certainly not surprising that Ruth's beliefs in a caring (and presumably interventionist) God were destroyed. The loss of her religion probably meant the loss of an important source of support and solace.

It has been suggested in the literature that those who cope best with trauma are those who have experienced a moderate amount of stress and trauma in the past. People who have had no trauma and those who have experienced a great deal have the toughest time coping with a new event. Ruth went from a rather sheltered life to one of extreme violence and pain. The only stressor of her childhood was dealt with, not by talking and confronting, but through withdrawal-avoidance and escape. From such a pattern one would not expect Ruth to tackle any new problems head-on.

In that Ruth was under constant threat of violence for an extended period of time, she might be expected to experience a more severe reaction than a single incident victim (e.g., rape victim). Multiple incident victims such as incest or child abuse victims and battered women exhibit similar symptoms and behavior patterns to Ruth. In fact, the self-mutilation exhibited by Ruth is commonly seen in abused incest victims. Alcohol or drug abuse are also common and suicide attempts are frequent. Such behavior patterns are desperate solutions to deal with "unspeakable" horrors all alone. Unfortunately, as is frequently seen in the case of incest, Ruth was actively discouraged from discussing what she had experienced. When the memories overwhelmed her, she would engage in whatever behavior was necessary to reduce the anxiety, even if it took the pain of a razor to bring her back to the present.

Re-experiencing an event through talking with others is an important part of recovery. Talking serves as a form of verbal desensitization whereby terrifying conditioned stimuli are experienced in a safe environment, facilitating extinction. I have found that this process resembles desensitization more than flooding in that victims describe to others only as much as they can cope with at a given time. Talking also helps the victim to change her/his faulty attributions about the world or the self. Social support is absolutely essential for the victim to feel protected during this process and for the victim to regain her self-esteem and belief that some people are good and to be trusted.

Unfortunately, probably because of her childhood pattern and the discouragement of her colleagues and prior therapist, Ruth did not have the opportunity to re-experience her traumas in a safe environment before they became established into a long-term pattern of overwhelming nightmares, flashbacks and chronic anxiety. Generalization has set in. Although she now has the opportunity to discuss these events with her various support groups, she does not have the ability to control her reactions. She also has an established pattern of avoiding discussion of these events and attempting to escape or avoid triggering cognitions.

ASSESSMENT QUESTIONS

My assessment of this client would focus on three areas, (1) general psychological functioning, (2) information about specific fears and fear reactions, and (3) social support. Because I have not conducted therapy with Viet Nam Veterans I would probably give her a few psychological assessment instruments in order to compare her with victims I am more knowledgeable about (i.e., rape victims, incest victims, battered women). I would ask her to complete the MMPI, the SCL-90, The Modified Fear Survey, the Impact of Events Scale, the Beck Depression Scale, and I would ask her to do some self-monitoring using the Emotion Thermometer for one week. If my hypothesis regarding Ruth's similarity to incest victims is correct, I would expect that she would have an invalid MMPI and that her F scale would be very elevated. I would also expect most of her clinical scales to be quite elevated. This pattern is a reflection of the extent of the life disruption experienced and the confusion and pain the client is experiencing. I would also be interested to see what pattern of fears she endorses on the Modified Fear Survey, and what her target fears for the Emotion Thermometer would be.

After confirming the information that I had received in this report, I would focus the interview next on the typology of her fear reactions. I would begin by giving her a brief overview of how fear is conditioned without using jargon, and would make some normalizing statements about typical fear reactions following trauma. I would then ask her to describe her fear reactions, her flashbacks and panic attacks, first in terms of how they feel to her subjectively, physically, then behaviorally, and finally what cognitions she has prior to fear reactions and during the panic attacks or flashbacks. I would ask Ruth to begin to identify stimuli, either environmental cues or cognitive cues, that currently trigger flashbacks and anxiety attacks. Before asking her to monitor these reactions, I would ask her to estimate the frequency of panic attacks, flashbacks, nightmares and so forth. I would ask her to rate the intensity of these experiences on a scale of 1 to 100.

I would ask Ruth to describe her typical coping strategies in both stimulus situations that she anticipates and those that she unexpectedly encounters. I would ask her to evaluate the relative effectiveness of her coping strategies. It would be important to build on any strategies that had at least partial success (except alcohol abuse). I would look for assets that we could build on and would like to know what strategies she's currently using to control her alcohol abuse. I would like to obtain information regarding the level of depression that Ruth is currently experiencing. The case study information indicates that Ruth is quite isolated socially, but I would like to know what reinforcers she currently has available, and if she is engaging in cognitions that facilitate depression (e.g., Beck's cognitive triad).

The third area of information I would like to have concerns social support. I would like to have more information regarding her relationships both in the past and currently. For instance, before her experiences in Viet Nam, did Ruth have women friends that she confided in? How close was she to family members? And did she draw upon available resources? After returning from Viet Nam, Ruth withdrew from most of her friends and family. I would like to know how they responded to her during this time, and how they reacted to her withdrawal. I would like to know more about her relationship with her sister. Is that relationship a source of social support? Do they have frequent contact? Is that relationship one that could be developed to help Ruth cope now?

I would be interested in exploring in a bit greater depth the relationship she had with the physician in Viet Nam. The case study material mentions that it was an abusive relationship. I would like to know more about the relationship, what the result of it was for Ruth and how it affected her abilities to develop and maintain heterosocial and heterosexual relationships. Ruth's list of goals does not mention the development of relationships. I would be interested to know whether friendships and intimacy are also goals. Finally, I would like to know whether she wished to return to nursing or if she had any other long term occupational goals for herself.

THERAPEUTIC STRATEGIES

I believe I might be able to meet her three goals in therapy: (1) to reduce her symptoms (2) to develop an understanding of her experiences and (3) to maintain sobriety. I would focus initially on the first of those goals and believe that with the reduction in fear and anxiety (flashbacks, nightmares, etc.), the other two goals would follow naturally. I believe that Ruth's primary problem is fear and anxiety. Alcohol abuse, depression and interpersonal difficulties are secondary to fear. Although there are several therapy techniques available to deal with this type of fear and anxiety problem, my preference is the use of stress inoculation. Systematic desensitization is helpful in the treatment of phobias, but individual hierarchies are necessary for each stimulus situation. Flooding has also been used recently with Viet Nam Veterans in order to extinguish flashbacks to specific traumatic events. However, like systematic desensitization, flooding does not generalize to new stimulus situations and the client does not learn the skill of fear management. Therefore, although I might use flooding at some point, I would begin by teaching Ruth fear management skills such as those taught in stress inoculation. Such a skills training approach would be valuable for Ruth to gain a sense of mastery over her experiences and would give her additional coping strategies for unexpected stimulus situations as well as those she has consciously avoided. Because stress inoculation is an active approach that emphasizes the client's ability to develop coping skills and mastery, it is very compatible with feminist theory. Such an approach allows the client to take charge of her life in a way that many of the passive talk therapies do not. However, the client's analysis of her role within a larger societal context would certainly augment stress inoculation training.

There are three major phases in stress inoculation training. The first phase is educational. The client is presented with the cognitive-behavioral formulation of the development and maintenance of trauma responses. In my work with rape victims, I have found that clients experience a great deal of relief when they realize that their fear reactions are logical and a conditioned response. Many women feel that they are going crazy and are out of control when they have anxiety attacks seemingly at random. During the educational phase, clients are taught to identify triggering stimuli that are present in the environment. Once Ruth is able to distinguish truly dangerous situations from conditioned, but nondangerous, situations she may feel somewhat calmer even before other training has begun.

The second phase of treatment is the skills building phase. It begins with progressive relaxation training. Given her chronic level of anxiety, it is likely that Ruth is in an almost constant state of sympathetic nervous system arousal. Therefore, she probably no longer remembers what it feels like to be truly relaxed. Progressive relaxation should focus on her particular tension spots and should include, not only muscular relaxation and deep breathing, but then cognitive relaxation using pleasant imagery. It may be necessary for Ruth to reconceptualize relaxation as an increase in control because she probably associates muscular tension with tight control. Therefore, for her to relax may seem like a loss of control initially. I would ask Ruth to practice relaxation several times a day and would ask her to attempt to use it when she has the urge to drink.

Once Ruth has learned how to relax herself, I would begin to teach her a briefer form of relaxation that she could use in stressful situations she encounters in daily living. I would first teach her diaphragmatic breathing and then would have her practice deep breathing paired with quick muscle relaxation such as dropping the shoulders, jaw and relaxing other muscle group we had identified as her trouble spots. I would encourage her to pick a relaxing image or phrase that she could draw upon quickly to help her feel calm and in control.

After brief relaxation is mastered, I would begin to teach other skills that can build on to it. For instance, for times when cognitions are out of control and a woman is ruminating or perseverating and can't seem to stop, I teach thought-stopping. For Ruth, the sequence might be thought-stopping then either progressive relaxation or brief relaxation depending upon the situation that she is in. If Ruth has problems refocusing her attention after using brief relaxation, I would probably teach her to use guided self-dialogue to focus on the task at hand or to analyze the situation she is in. When I work with women who have been raped, I teach them to analyze the dangerousness of the stimulus situation *after* they have used brief relaxation, because even if they are in danger, it is important that they calm themselves first so that they can decide how to handle the situation. If it is an old, conditioned, but nondangerous situation, they stay in that environ-

ment until they feel calm. I would probably use the same
approach with Ruth and ask her if, for instance, she heard an
explosion or heard or saw a helicopter, that she use brief
relaxation and then use guided self-dialogue to remind herself
to relax and stay in that situation, to look at the helicopter
and remind herself that she is no longer in danger. Hopefully,
she would be able to use these techniques prior to and during
flashbacks to her Viet Nam experiences.

If there were situations she was avoiding because they were
likely to trigger flashbacks or anxiety reactions, I would teach
her how to set up hierarchies and how to use cognitive rehearsal prior to actively encountering any of the steps of the hierarchy. Cognitive rehearsal should be realistic in that Ruth
could imagine herself becoming somewhat anxious or starting
to feel tension and then using the brief relaxation or some of
the other skills to cope with that tension and anxiety. If any of
hierarchy steps are interpersonal, behavioral rehearsal may
prove beneficial.

Once Ruth has acquired these coping skills, I would then
consider the possibility of some flooding sessions for some of
the difficult flashbacks. Because Ruth is not likely to encounter similar situations in her normal environment, many of
these flashbacks would remain untouched with the coping
skills strategy.

I believe that the therapy strategy I have suggested would
help reduce Ruth's fear and anxiety reactions. However, I
think that these techniques would also provide her with some
viable alternatives to alcohol use during stressful times. Relaxation can be practiced at night to help induce sleep while
the other techniques can be implemented in both fear produc-
ing situations and difficult interpersonal encounters.

Because of her isolation, I would spend a fair amount of
therapy time helping Ruth to reestablish former relationships
and to develop new ones. I might have to begin by helping
her restructure her attitudes regarding self-disclosure and social support. I suspect that her self-esteem is so poor that she
would have trouble receiving friendship as well as giving it.
Assertion training could prove beneficial in allowing Ruth to
ask for what she needs from others and in preventing the
development of abusive relationships like the one she experienced with the physician in Viet Nam.

Finally, I would encourage her to continue with her support groups. I am a strong advocate of group therapy for recovery from victimization. Because victimization is often an isolating experience, people frequently feel that their reactions are unique or particularly bad. Hearing about similarities in feelings and reactions from others can be reassuring. Furthermore, group members can support each other's new coping strategies. I have found that in behavioral groups for rape victims or incest survivors, the group members influence each other as they practice new skills. If someone is reluctant to attempt a new technique or to practice skills at home, the success of other members encourages the reluctant member through modeling. Everyone progresses faster in the supportive environment of a group.

On a more general level, I would suggest two things to prevent such distress in future generations of women. First, stress inoculation was developed originally as a prevention technique. Women who have not experienced trauma could and should learn coping strategies and skills to reduce anxiety. Women are particularly vulnerable to fear reactions. Rather then merely accepting this fact as inevitable and therefore trying to shelter girls and women, we should be helping them to develop positive coping strategies before they are subjected to stress. Second, people should not be blamed for victimization and expected to cope with traumas all alone. Some events in life are too big for one person to handle all by herself. Because most people appear to subscribe to the "stiff upper lip" philosophy of life, people are often criticized for reacting strongly and recovering "too slowly" from traumas. Perhaps our own fears of death and inadequacy prevent us from being supportive. However, we need to provide support for extended periods of time when someone has experienced life-threatening traumas. And we all need to become aware of the magnitude of distress that is caused by some of life's tragic events.

I hope that Ruth has now found a supportive environment where she feels accepted and where she is encouraged to develop new skills and to reclaim her self-esteem. And although she has experienced intensely the horrors of war, I hope she can now find some peace in her world.

Perspective of a Sex Therapist

Lorna J. Sarrel

When I was asked to comment on Ruth's story from the point of view of a sex therapist, I was inclined to refuse since there is so little data about her sexuality and, indeed, at this point in her treatment, sex seems irrelevant. I changed my mind because I reflected on the all too common neglect of sexual issues by therapists. I think it is worthwhile to raise therapists' awareness of sexual issues and to reinforce the idea that sex is a legitimate area of therapeutic intervention.

Sexual concerns are obviously not at the top of the priority list in view of Ruth's severely impaired functioning and her alcoholism. However, if one takes an optimistic view and extends the treatment goals to include a plan for therapy after the initial three goals have been achieved, then it would seem appropriate to talk with the client about her sexual history and learn whether she would want to try to include sexual relationships in her life once more.

What we know of Ruth's sexual history is that she "dated" in age-appropriate ways and was engaged to a man with whom she "petted" but did not have intercourse because of religious scruples. We have no data on her level of enjoyment or her feelings about these experiences but the case-history seems to imply that at least there were no major sexual traumas or problems until the relationship with the married doctor in Da Nang.

Ruth describes this relationship as sexually and emotionally abusive. That sounds like a stark contrast with the loving, mutually agreed upon sexual intimacy Ruth had experienced with her fiancé. I assume that, as Ruth herself tells us, her need to have "someone to depend on and be protected by"

Lorna Sarrel, M.S.W., is co-director of the Yale University Human Sexuality Program.

was so great that she chose to put up with abuse rather than lose a "protector."

Ruth also says that she was naive about normative expectations for a relationship. I am speculating, but I imagine that she means at least some of the following concerns:

1. Can a man legitimately demand sex whenever he needs it, whether or not I am in the mood?
2. If he has an erection, is it my obligation to "relieve" him?
3. If my partner wants to do things, e.g. fellatio, which I don't enjoy, do I have the right to refuse?
4. Is it normal for intercourse to be painful?
5. Should I feel pleasure and have an orgasm during intercourse?

These questions normally arise in the course of early sexual relationships. Given a normal environment and a loving partner, they can usually be resolved. In Ruth's situation, I imagine that there was little or no possibility for dealing with these nuances. I have a mental picture of Ruth and the doctor, stealing an hour in bed with the sound of helicopters and distant explosions in the background. I also imagine an unexpressed "contract"; the doctor would provide holding and a temporary sense of safety and Ruth would provide sex—no questions asked. We don't know if the doctor was actually sadistic or merely insensitive but the end result for Ruth was the same. She felt sexually and emotionally abused.

Most women have difficulty asserting their sexual needs or simply saying "ouch" when something hurts. Given Ruth's socialization and her extreme neediness in a terrifying, emotionally stressful situation, it is not surprising that she was helpless to assert or protect herself.

Since there was no mention of any relationship with a man subsequent to the doctor, it is likely that Ruth became very frightened about the prospect of any sexual intimacy and has simply avoided it by avoiding relationships with men. As she improves in therapy, this may become more apparent. And, should she venture into an emotional relationship with a man, she might well encounter "irrational" panic at any point. Sex therapists call this sexual aversion; it is the recurrence of phobic anxiety in sexual or potentially sexual situations. This could, perhaps, be worked through in individual therapy or, if she was in a fairly stable relationship, the couple could be referred for sex therapy. It is my impression that Ruth would benefit from a discussion of her sexual anxieties with her therapist fairly soon because she may be unable to take even the first steps toward a relationship with a man until some of these anxieties are addressed. It is, of course, important to keep in mind that Ruth may be comfortable with celibacy. I think the appropriate stance of the therapist would be to respect Ruth's goals for herself but to at least point out that comfortable and satisfying sexual behavior might be possible for her.

The therapist should also be aware that Ruth's experiences with the doctor may have affected how she feels about doctors in general and/or about gynecological exams. If she is afraid of such an examination, the therapist can help to pave the way by making a referral to a sensitive doctor, mid-wife or nurse practitioner and, if the patient gives permission, talking in advance to the person who will do the examination. One should anticipate that Ruth may have vaginismus (involuntary tensing of the vaginal muscles) with any attempt at vaginal penetration, including a pelvic exam.

On a more philosophical note, I would like to add the thought that sexuality is such an important dimension of personality that *no* therapy can be considered whole which excludes it from consideration. It is not implausible that Ruth's social isolation is intensified, perhaps even caused, by her fears of sex and her sense of herself as sexually inadequate. Sadness about not bearing children, as her biological time clock ticks on, could also be an unspoken but deep source of pain. At some point in her therapy—and probably sooner rather than later—Ruth's sexuality should be discussed. Otherwise, the therapist recapitulates a negative experience from her childhood—the experience of feeling alone with her sexual thoughts because they are too "bad" or too embarrassing to be discussed openly.

Alcoholism First

Michelle Clark

This is a poignant story. It also makes me angry. It is poignant to see this well-meaning young woman lose her sense of self to war and alcoholism. It is infuriating to hear that she was not taken seriously or cared for properly when she complained of a real physical illness. Infuriating to learn that a psychiatrist prescribed daily Valium for someone worried about her drinking. Valium potentiates addiction to alcohol. So her psychiatrist was, literally, physically, making her illness worse. He didn't take seriously her concerns about her drinking, didn't work on the unresolved wartime stress which had started her drinking. I can only suppose, then, that he ignored her adult life and self and went straight to childhood reminiscences and stayed there. He focused, perhaps (we are not told), on the defects in her upbringing (perhaps in her mother), but probably never asked about parental alcoholism. He did not address her genuine adult confusion and pain. This is unfortunate for many reasons, but the crucial one is that he might have aided her facing her alcoholism in its early stage when she still had her self-esteem, a profession and was in contact with her family and friends.

Though it is infuriating to hear about this mistreatment, it is not surprising. Rare is the mental health training program which teaches about alcoholism and its accompanying family syndrome. Most mental health professionals learn about alcoholism once they are working in the field. Many never learn about it. Many mental health professionals are ignorant of alcoholism and, therefore, treat men and women for other symp-

Michelle Clark, M.Ed., is a staff psychotherapist at the Women's Mental Health Collective, Inc. in Somerville, Massachusetts. She is on the editorial board of *Women & Therapy* and has taught, most recently, in the Adult Degree Program of Norwich University. She has written about women's history and literature for The Feminist Press, *Seven Days* magazine and other periodicals.

toms (depression, for example), which cannot be changed before sobriety and, in some cases, disappear with sobriety.

In women alcoholism is even less likely to be diagnosed because of the social stigma attached to a female who drinks. Our society considers it sad but acceptable for a woman to be depressed or hysterical, but unacceptable and disgusting to be a female and drunk. Until very recently there were no special services for women alcoholics. Even now such services are the exception. Alcoholics Anonymous (AA), although it has helped many women attain sobriety, has also had an implicitly male style and many women have not been able to reach out to it for help. For example, Bill W., one of the founders of AA called "the average alcoholic, self-centered in the extreme,"[1] likely to think of himself as invulnerable, always right, always in control. A man who habitually thinks of his own good before the good of others. AA was started by men. Its particular mixture of support and confrontation developed to heal such self-centered men. But a woman alcoholic might be the opposite kind of person; overly solicitous of others, habitually putting herself last. Some of the self-critical aspects of AA might make a woman with low self-esteem feel even more worthless, and she would not be able to stay with the program. Fortunately, in some areas of the country, recovering women alcoholics are making changes in the AA style.

Ruth received her care from the Veterans Administration, an agency designed to serve men. I would expect it to be backward in its ideas about how to care for women. In Ruth's case it exhibits a typical kind of medical sexism. Every problem the woman had was in her head.

Though this story touches me, I would not see Ruth in individual psychotherapy at the setting where I currently work which is a licensed free-standing clinic which has a twenty-four hour answering service but no hospital affiliation and no walk-in services. I don't understand why she was released from the hospital when she is "actively suicidal."

If she came to me for treatment I would suggest that she either seek a day treatment program or individual psychotherapy at an institution which had a twenty-four hour walk-in service and, also, a specialty in alcoholism.

Ruth needs a lot of daily life re-learning and unintense but continuous interpersonal contact to begin to rebuild her sense of herself. There is no adult ego inside her right now. Inside, one part of her is a fearful, overwhelmed child (her hallucinations and nightmare); the other part of her is an angry, avenging conscience (her suicidal ideation, self-mutilation, chronic tearfulness).

Her alcoholism is at the end of the middle stage, the beginning of the last stage. In the middle stage of alcoholism the person has had many job difficulties, cut off ties with family and friends, drinks in the morning. In the last stage, the person has undefinable fears, is unable to concentrate, feels hopeless, depressed and guilty. Before she can deal with her war experiences Ruth needs to feel calmer inside. She should be attending one AA or aftercare meeting every day. Some of these meetings should be for women only. In my clinical experience many women find they can form minimally trusting relationships earlier and easier in an all women's sobriety or support group.

Ruth has, at this point, completely lost her ability to soothe herself. Self-soothing is the internalized capacity to be a good mother to yourself. It is the capacity to have a feeling, bear it without denying it and know that it will pass. Perhaps her inner capacity to soothe herself was never very developed.

Ruth's feeling of self-worth as a child and a young adult came from being a good girl. She was, as she reports, "a good daughter," popular, achieving, a good caretaker. She didn't make waves. Her parents and other important adults approved of her. Her friends approved of her. She believed in a caring God who, if she were good, would also approve of her. And she *was* good. She didn't cause problems. Therefore she received approval and felt good about herself. A nursing career consolidated her identity as a person who gets her self-esteem by taking care of others. Many women live their whole lives with such an identity. While this identity has its problems and limitations, if Ruth had not gone to war she might never have been pressed past her own limits.

In the war zone, Ruth's caretaking behaviors which had won her approval and self esteem, did not give her inner satisfaction or an outer sense of doing well. She was not able to see people healing under her care which was, for her, a central source of adult competence. Perhaps her superiors were too busy and stressed themselves to praise the job she was doing. She did not, perhaps, know how to get angry or think critically (I don't know for sure, there is not enough information), which might have provided her with an emotional outlet during this stressful time. Since the "expectation was held by her colleagues that none of them would discuss feelings about working in a war zone," Ruth had nowhere to turn to explore the stress she was experiencing. The only socially acceptable soother, in the war zone, was alcohol, and so, Ruth, like many others, turned to it.

Ruth was, initially, suffering from stress when she turned to alcohol to soothe herself. But at this point, fifteen years later, Ruth's primary illness is middle-to-late stage alcoholism, her secondary problem is delayed posttraumatic stress disorder. The symptoms of these two illnesses have similarities: depression, inability to feel, inability to concentrate, recurrent nightmares, powerful but non-specific feelings of guilt and foreboding.

Ruth's task is to rebuild her capacity to soothe herself without using alcohol and then decide what she feels, thinks and wants to do about the terrible events she witnessed.

Three months of sobriety on an inpatient unit is a beginning. The most effective method for rebuilding the inner capacity to soothe the self is the consistent support of people on the same road. Viet Nam veterans who have been addicted and are further along in their recovery will be very helpful to Ruth. As will any women who're recovering alcoholics. Genuine identification with others is crucial for rebuilding Ruth's inner capacity to calm herself. Support from people is put in the place of alcohol. A woman AA sponsor, who will be on call for Ruth whenever she needs to talk, would be beneficial.

In this process, the individual psychotherapist is a peripheral person. The therapist can be another helping person who teaches about soothing, reaching out to others and encourages Ruth to take good care of herself. The danger is that the therapist becomes the person whom Ruth feels "really helps, really understand," while Ruth continues to isolate herself. This is the danger of individual psychotherapy in early sobriety—the therapist is idealized and the efforts of the AA sponsor, AA group members and veterans group members are denigrated. This would slow rather than facilitate Ruth's recovery.

At this point, the war memories have become the excuse for Ruth's drinking. She blames the war, the memories and the flashbacks for how bad she's feeling, why she needs a drink. But these traumas will be resolved, first, by relearning the soothing process and, second, learning to show anger productively, think critically, ask questions. Ruth might, eventually, become a person whose development is enhanced by a "survivor mission," helping other Viet Nam vets and nurses organize for recognition and reparations for service-connected injuries.

When Ruth has stopped feeling suicidal and self-mutilating and has had a year or more uninterrupted sobriety and participation in AA, individual therapy could become more useful to her. Once she is unlikely to isolate herself, individual therapy will provide *additional* education in what feelings are, how to bear them, how to struggle with pain, how to say no to the demands of others. The individual therapist would add support to the self-soothing process AA had begun. Ruth's long range task would be to learn to have a self which exists for itself as well as to take care of others.

When Ruth is feeling stronger inside she might want to explore, with her therapist, her family history. I wonder if either of her parents were alcoholic. If one or both of them were, then, her turn to alcohol under stress was, in part, a learned behavior. Parental alcoholism also increases the likelihood that Ruth did not receive enough soothing in her childhood. Once she is sober for a year or more, talking about family alcoholism will help Ruth put into perspective her own drinking and her own, earlier, adaptive, self-protective good-girl behaviors.

Alcoholism is the most common addictive illness in our society. Preventative alcohol education should be a part of school curricula from grade school through high school. Good alcohol education is not moralistic. It differentiates between safe and problem drinking and introduces young people to resources which might help them if they are having a problem with their own or a parent's drinking.

I do not believe it is possible to do away with war or a standing army. Therefore, I think alcohol education and stress management education should be ongoing in the Armed Forces. Alcoholism, like stress-related illness, if caught early, is more amenable to treatment. Ruth might, eventually, be a person who lobbied for such programs.

The Interplay of Individual Psychodynamics and the Female Experience: A Case Study

Amy B. Ryberg

A feminist-psychodynamic orientation to conceptualizing a woman's personality and to engaging in psychotherapy with her involves the wedding of two rather disparate philosophical views. Psychodynamic therapy, with its emphasis on individual pathology and personality organization, looks at the individual's history and her *perception* of that history. It focuses on the developmental tasks of childhood and significant relationships as the primary forces shaping the personality. A psychodynamic perspective need not adhere strictly to the precepts of Freudian thought such as drive theory and the primacy of bodily zones as related to instinct, conflict, and resolution (via sublimation, integration, or symptom formation). Incorporating these notions, psychodynamism also looks at object-relations theory (Winnicott, in Davis & Walbridge, 1984), to explain both "healthy" and "pathological" personality function. The quality of the individual's early interactions is seen as crucial in working through such issues as trust, dependency, and intimacy. What a psychodynamic perspective *does* necessarily include is a belief in the crucial importance of experiences of childhood and adolescence in building a foundation of perceptions about the self, important relationships, and the world at large. The child's *experience* of nurturance, trust, autonomy, loss, etc. becomes the core of his/her personality, and further life experiences are accretions of this, much as building

Amy B. Ryberg, M.S.W., is a clinical social worker in private practice at East Pointe Mental Health Center. She has devoted the last three years to having a baby, Benjamin, and she bore him with joy and relief on February 23, 1985.

a house necessarily depends on the quality and nature of its foundation. Involved in this is the idea that each person processes his/her experience personally and uniquely. In the process of raising my infant son, who has very much loved to be held and cuddled literally since birth, I have come across two utterly disparate approaches to my gratification of this: (1) he is not learning to be alone, is too dependent on me and needs me for security rather than developing this internally, and is being "spoiled"; (2) a small child, under two years of age, cannot be held and cuddled too much, and this develops a sense of security from which he will then be able to separate himself and become autonomous. Having spent much time and anxiety attempting to resolve this and similar issues, I am struck not only with the obvious fact that the answers aren't in, but that the *meaning* of being held, to my son, will greatly influence the outcome. A corollary to this is that the child's meaning may be different or antithetical to the adult's perception of the events or interactions, and also to the adult's intentions as to how the child would perceive these.

Psychodynamic thought does retain the primacy of some Freudian beliefs such as the existence and importance of the unconscious, the function of defense mechanisms, the function of dreams, and the idea that all new development is influenced to varying degrees by how the child has previously developed. Even though more eclectic psychodynamic thought de-emphasizes some of the more orthodox Freudian beliefs, it retains a belief in the basic *processes* of personality development. That is, it may refute many of the conclusions Freudians arrive at as to the *meaning* of a person's conflicts and strivings, while retaining a belief that the developmental processes and experiences *are* crucial in understanding a person's behavior, thought, and emotional experience (Eichenbaum & Orbach, 1983).

I use traditional psychoanalytic language because I feel it is technically precise, although I am aware of, and agree with, feminist concerns about language which may subtly discredit the patient or which may be value-laden. My use of these terms is neutral and value-free, and describes observable clinical phenomena. Likewise, when conceptualizing a psychodynamic approach to psychotherapy, key analytic concepts and practices are retained, such as repetition compulsion, resistance, analysis of dream material, importance of free association (to varying degrees), and transference and countertransference. I prefer to understand the latter as the nature of therapeutic relationships—what goes on between therapist and client, and what it *means* to each, within the context of the life experiences of each. That is, a psychodynamic treatment approach involves understanding and interpreting the client's difficulties in terms of repetition of patterns of perceptions, feelings, and relationships, partly in an attempt to master or resolve conflict, and partly because this is the organization that this person imposes on the various events and relationships of his/her life. Because of this, some degree of neutrality and non-directiveness is necessary as a therapeutic technique, so that the client can impose his/her own order and meaning on the process of therapy.

Feminist theory and practice, in contrast, involve sociological, political, economic and historic perspectives. Necessarily, they focus on commonly experienced values, expectations, and behaviors held by parts (or the entirety) of society at large. They are based on the idea that women share commonly held values, experiences, role prescriptions and proscriptions *because of their sex* (Miller, 1976). Obviously, this is also true of men. The notion is that one's sex is a major cultural and psychological determinant of one's experiences, expectations, opportunities, privileges, restrictions, on both a sociological and a personal psychological level. It is based on an understanding of all aspects of the feminine experience—biological, psychological, and socio-economic, as these impact on women as a population group. An important notion, in my understanding of feminist theory, is the idea that socio-economic roles and privileges, and psychological organization of percepts of reality are determined by one's sex and by how society transmits attitudes, beliefs, and values about that sex. In other words, there are the biological realities of femaleness: menstruation, pregnancy, child-bearing and lactation, as well as (usually) smaller physical stature, less physical strength for short-term activities (as opposed to physical stamina) and other effects of the female hormones on body function and capabilities. Beyond these (which are still open to raging debate, such as the effect of menstruation and hormones on mental and emotional functioning), are the psychological and social experiences females uniquely encounter in this culture. These not only shape opportunity, (e.g., economically and politically), but also shape psychology—one's perceptions of oneself in relation to the world, one's values, sense of self-determination, conflict, etc. There seems to be an emotional back-and-forth flow of these from individual woman to culture and back to individual woman; the personal reinforcing the cultural and vice versa.

Feminist theory emphasizes the idea that these cultural archetypes or unconscious universal beliefs (Bolen, 1984), and economics and politics (very conscious policies, privileges, and restrictions), greatly influence not only woman's functioning in the marketplace and the corridors of power, but also influence in rather universal and predictable ways, a woman's psychological development and personality organization. Thus, a particular value held by a woman (e.g., nurturing and care-giving) may be understood not only in terms of her own personal life experiences, but also as a truth commonly expected of and valued in women. Conceptualization of a particular conflict a woman brings to therapy is enhanced by understanding of these issues peculiar to women. I find this particularly important in understanding modes of functioning and organizing of reality which have to do with the female experience. For example, I recently heard a radio program comparing the meaning of identical behavior in men and women in the office: if a man has pictures of his family on his desk, he is seen as a sober family man, whereas a woman having the same pictures implies less seriousness of purpose about career—her "heart is really at home."

There are two distinct key themes in feminist psychology: (1) that various facets of society serve to maintain women's powerlessness economically and politically, so as to not threaten the male status quo (e.g., women's property rights being separate from that of their husband's, women's access to roles of power in business and government); and (2) that one's identity as woman, and experience as woman, shapes the expectations, experiences, and perceptions of society, and of each individual woman. This latter point is where feminist theory most clearly intersects with psychodynamic understanding—an emphasis on the individual's experience and the meaning this has for her. However, feminism adds the notion that a great deal of the meaning is: (1) universal to women; and (2) frequently used consciously or unconsciously to be psychologically, emotionally or politically oppressive (or at least limiting), due simply to the *fact* of femaleness.

Much psychological theory has also contributed to this oppression, this view of women as "abnormal, immature, neurotic," by conceptualizing women's functioning in terms of what is considered normal, healthy, and mature for men. Women, needless to say, frequently fall short of being "normal males." Feminist theory explores and emphasizes the nature of women—women's values, perceptions, etc. and understands women's functioning and women's problems in these terms (Gilligan, 1982).

Feminist therapy, then, focuses on interpreting these facts to women and embarking on an understanding of how these previously mentioned factors strongly influence women's perceptions of reality—their sense of conflict and of possibility, how they understand their own psyches and their relationship to society. In some ways this enlarges on the psychodynamic process by exploring individual meaning and reaction (here, the meaning of being female), but it diverges by elaborating on cultural themes such as nurturance, relatedness, etc., and by pointing out how and why the culture does this. That is, the individual woman is not merely experiencing her own unique neurosis, though she certainly is living with her own perception of reality, but she is also reacting to very real, powerful, external forces which most or all women must contend with. She is not simply defeating herself; but is reacting to cultural forces whose aim it is to define and limit her, and to a culture and a psychological establishment which rejects feminine values and labels them as immature or neurotic. For example, female relatedness tends to be seen as a problem of separation—individualization (Gilligan, 1982; Miller, 1976).

Obviously, it can be quite conflictual for the therapist to weed through the client's material and sort all this out. What is largely a personal, emotional problem for the client, and what is a reaction to the condition of women can certainly be a judgment call. Most issues have some of both elements, as elaborated by the purely psychodynamic approach (cure the individual's conflicts and she will be okay), or by the purely socio-political approach (change society and she will be okay), but a feminist-psychodynamic approach believes in an interplay of the two, with contributions from each source varying with the issues and with the woman. In such an integrative approach the therapist needs to understand all these different factors, and to maintain a somewhat different therapeutic stance. At times, the neutrality and non-directiveness of the dynamic approach need to give way to an activist approach, such as educating the woman as to these factors and encouraging her to try behaviors which have political implications in terms of breaking through sexual roles and changing power relationships, and engaging in a relationship of sisterhood—of both client and therapist being foremost women, sharing and valuing common experiences of being women in this culture, and attempting to negotiate these in our daily functioning and in our private psychological realities.

In addressing the case of Ruth, I attempted to integrate the two schools of thought and practice previously delineated. I sense Ruth as having some predisposition to difficulties in coping with emotional problems, though not sufficient to explain her present level of disintegration, based on the case material. This will be discussed further.

Early on, she developed a style of withdrawal to deal with unpleasant emotions. The unacceptability of dealing with feelings was reinforced by her Viet Nam colleagues not talking about their experiences, and by her psychiatrist when he, too, discouraged her dealing with these. This is certainly a repetition of her early relationships with her parents, where she was not encouraged to express and work through her unacceptable feelings and to be compliant. It is similarly a feminist issue of unequal power relationships (male-female; doctor-patient; parent-child) and reiterates the professional doctor-nurse relationship within which she was socialized. Her style of dealing with her feelings is a precursor of alcohol abuse and may be significant in the doubting of her own perception of reality. If a child cannot deal openly with feelings in the family context, not only are feelings deemed unacceptable, but the child *herself* feels unacceptable or bad for having those feelings ("my feelings and I are identical"), and the child has no way to explore the reality of her perceptions. This phenomenon is full-blown in Ruth's questioning of whether her symptoms are "real," and in her acceptance of serious medical misdiagnosis. Unfortunately, alcohol abuse enhances a sense of unreality. This is central to the nature of addiction. "A person repeatedly feels artificial infusions of a sensation . . . that is not supplied by the organic balance of his life as a whole. Such infusions insulate him from the fact that the world he perceives psychologically is becoming farther and farther removed from the real state of his body or his life" (Peele, 1975, p. 47). Ruth experiences many dichotomies as to what reality to trust: drunk-sober, nightmares-awake, emotions-facts, psychiatrist's-her own, and has lost the moorings of her religious beliefs. This central problem of withdrawal, and of inability to explore one's perceptions is a recurrent theme in Ruth's life.

Ruth seems not to have had her own dependency needs gratified appropriately and, instead, to have been reinforced for being a "junior mother." This is a good example of the intersection of feminist and psychodynamic thinking, for it is a typically female experience to deny one's own dependency and to feel one should be fulfilled by giving to others, while it is also a psychodynamic problem in terms of shame and guilt over one's unacceptable, unmet needs and the felt necessity of keeping them repressed and attempting to gratify them in indirect (e.g., identification with the recipient of one's own care) or harmful (the affair with the physician) ways. Ruth's early experiences are punctuated with unmet needs, unacceptability of anger, and the idea that one must be seriously nonfunctional in order to receive attention and nurturance. The latter is reiterated by the severe debilitation of the soldiers, and herself in her alcoholism. Her conflicts over her wishes to be dependent and nurtured, and her guilt at this, further enhance her conflicts as to whether she *really* needs psychiatric attention or whether she is just "making it up." The only other way to get nurturance, in her relationship with the doctor, is to have sex. This is a theme common in women's lives—the exchanging of sex for closeness. The abusiveness, and her tolerance of it, seem to be her punishment for needing "someone to depend on and be protected by," or at least the necessary price to pay. Nurturance isn't available freely. She has handled her dependency needs via withdrawal, denial, drug use (alcohol and Valium), reaction formation via competency and care-giving, and identification with the recipients of her care.

I suspect she may also feel quite powerless and may experience a severe loss of self-esteem due to her experiences in nurturance with her sister and the soldiers, where the outcomes were so hopeless. That is, her efforts and abilities did not generally result in the recipients' improvement. Both her nightmares of the soldiers hurting her and her own suicidal attempts involving self-mutilation, seem to express her anger at herself for not being able to nurture back to health. They also may reinforce the dangers of neediness or dependency—getting nurtured doesn't really help; she should give up wishing for it.

In understanding Ruth there appear to be some serious gaps in the presenting history. As discussed, there are certainly predisposing factors in her roles of daughter and nurse, in her lack of gratification of dependency needs, and in her style of dealing with feelings via withdrawal and denial. However, there is an enormous discrepancy between her functioning pre and post Viet Nam. Her history in no way explains or predicts the extent of her decompensation. A more thorough history, focusing on psychological functioning, needs to be obtained. This would especially need to focus on how she processes her perceptions, use of defense mechanisms, sense of self, ability to regulate conflict and tension, and family relationships, including any family history of alcoholism. Certainly, Ruth is experiencing Post-Traumatic Stress Syndrome and alcoholism, both of which add variables not predicted by her history. Indeed, it is possible that had Ruth not experienced Viet Nam, she would not be currently suffering to this extreme. The intensity and duration of her symptoms (the hallucinations, self-mutilation, and active suicidal thoughts) bespeak underlying emotional conflict, ego deficits, and unresolved issues (c.f. Scarf, 1980). That is, I identify Viet Nam as the precipitating variable in Ruth's life, with underlying predisposing factors lying vulnerably and tentatively in wait for stressors to unleash them. Ruth is not suffering *only* from Post-Traumatic Stress Syndrome. She is experiencing an individual reaction to particular experiences and to the meaning of these experiences within the framework of her pre-morbid personality organization. Ruth needs to be understood and helped in this context. There is a core depression. Her symptoms describe a loss of self alternating numbness and emotional isolation with pervasive anxiety and use of self-mutilation to discharge affect and to experience her internal self. This is a psychotic depression with much attendant decompensation of reality testing, personality integration, object relations, and hallucinations. Something is missing from the case discussion presented—something to explain the ego dissolution Ruth is experiencing. The fact that she is ambivalent about treatment may be an entrée. What is she ambivalent about: whether she needs it, whether it will help, whether it is acceptable to be troubled and/or dependent? Based on her current functioning, excluding the extreme effects of Post-Traumatic Stress Syndrome, I begin to question her early functioning. Perhaps she held herself together with external structures—family roles, the teachings of the Catholic Church in her religious and academic experiences, the Navy. Perhaps her "goodness" consisted of compliance and an obsessive-compulsive style (Shapiro, 1965), of adaptation. Perhaps her living at home until age twenty-three, being so good and so helpful, without any sexual experience, bespeak an incomplete resolution of issues of differentiation of identity. She may have merged her ego, in terms of both identity and regulatory functions, with her environment so that she was able to function well with this support, but disintegrated when severe stress, combined with lack of external support and structure, occurred. This notion is supported by her lack of appropriate dependency satisfaction, and her emotional isolation at the time of beginning therapy, her fears of satisfying her need and wish to be dependent. In other words, even though she may have been allowed to be appropriately childlike, she may have depended on the structure of her family, and on her religious and social environments to provide the integration so that she could function so well prior to her Viet Nam experience. This dependency foreshadows her alcoholism . . . "it (addiction) gives their lives a structure and secures them, at least subjectively, against the press of what is novel and demanding" (Peele, 1975, p. 45).

The feminist issues here seem to be of the two types discussed earlier. First there are the historical, psychodynamic issues which have to do with feminine roles, expectations, and need. Ruth was expected to function as a "junior mother," and was reinforced for so doing. This pattern of self-sacrifice, denial of one's own needs and one's anger about this pattern, and reward for nurturance, is typically female. So is Ruth's choice of a nursing career which reiterates this pattern, and reinforces her underlying neediness and dependency. The excessive, early, unrealistic responsibility does not generally help a child feel competent. Instead, she experiences herself as "in over her head," and any successes on her part feel ego-alien—flukes, not coming from her own abilities. In Ruth's case, this is exacerbated by her actual experiences as a care-giver of her sister and the soldiers, people who are not going to "get better." This would likely reinforce her sense of powerlessness and ineffectiveness. Her efforts are guaranteed *not* to help her feel competent, or to enhance any sense of mastery. All this creates a sense of pseudo-autonomy, marked by an ability to function at high levels with no corresponding inner sense of strength. Her alcoholism further exacerbates this and, indeed, reaffirms these internal feelings. She has been alcoholic for thirteen years—since age twenty-six. She hasn't accomplished the developmental tasks of adulthood—separation, formation of some deep, rewarding relationships, and formation of a solid identity and set of values, and has, in fact, lost her solid religious beliefs. She is stultified, and the gap between her age and her functioning is growing.

The relationships in which she does experience any nurturance are abusive. She feels she must tolerate her lover's treatment of her, and she endures, with her internist and her psychiatrist, significant misunderstanding and medical malpractice in obtaining care for her tuberculosis and her psychiatric problems. Again, this is a pattern reinforced in women; that women should be care-givers, not care-receivers, that they must pay a high price to receive care, and that they feel conflicted, guilty, and ashamed when receiving care—as if they are being manipulative, deceitful, exaggerating, greedy, histrionic, etc.

Second are the socio-political experiences encountered by Ruth, and reinforced by the culture as normative. In this category would fall her experiences with hospitalization. She is diagnosed, unbelievably for two years, as having psychosomatic symptomatology, when, in fact, she has tuberculosis. This assumption, by the medical establishment, of physical symptoms as all being "in a woman's head," that all women are neurotic, oversensitive, etc., is a bias unique to women. Men are generally seen as sober and responsible, not prone to "emotionality" and their complaints are dealt with as such. In fact, the reverse is often true of men. The medical establishment tends to underdiagnose psychosomatic and psychogenic illness in men. I would wonder how Ruth reacted to this misdiagnosis and mistreatment, whether she passively accepted it and allowed this to further her lack of trust in her own perceptions of reality, or whether she questioned this, asked for opinions, etc. Again, it is a female stance to assume that the doctor, men, the establishment (here all embodied in her psychiatrists), know better than she and that they will be angry if she questions them. Apart from the obvious, gross malpractice and incompetence of her psychiatrist in ignoring her alcoholism and discouraging talk about her feelings, prescribing large, long-term doses of tranquilizers is a "treatment approach" much more frequently experienced by female than male patients. All these horrible experiences reinforce passivity, compliance, little-girl dependency, and increasing amounts of self-doubt and alienation, which circularly reinforce the passivity and compliance. This also describes the downward spiral of addiction. These are issues experienced by many women in dealing with the medical establishment. The psychiatric establishment is also problematic, as it tends to identify the above-described traits (passivity, etc.) as normal in women.

If Ruth were my patient, I would strongly encourage her to maintain her support group programs. The Viet Nam veterans group would hopefully encourage not only an expression of feeling, but also a sharing and affirmation of experience and perception. I would not only support AA participation, but would particularly encourage a women's AA group if this were available, to support and explore problems and perceptions of women alcoholics. That is, the group would deal with alcoholism, provide a vehicle for exploration and support of her experience of reality as common to other women and to other alcoholics, and encourage Ruth to begin to form connections to other people to break through her isolation. Also, the connectedness with people is an important nurturing, therapeutic experience.

In terms of psychotherapy, I would use the feminist-psychodynamic modality previously discussed to deal with those issues not touched by the various support groups; most notably, the meaning of her life events and her reactions to them. To address Ruth's needs, I would employ a dual focus of un-covering/interpretative and ego-building psychotherapy. That is, Ruth needs to explore her conflicts regarding dependency, neediness, anger, care-giving, and identity, but she also needs to develop more flexible and sophisticated ego strengths to deal with these and with the demands of her life, rather than to use avoidance, denial, intellectualization, alcohol, and regression into psychosis. Long-term psychotherapy would offer Ruth a warm, supportive relationship within the context of a "holding environment" (Davis and Wallbridge, 1981), in which she could derive enough care and use the ego-supports of the therapist and the therapeutic environment not only to explore her conflicts, but also to experiment with and internalize her own self-regulatory mechanisms, such as expression of anger and need, and trusting of her perceptions. Obviously, it is crucial to eventually move beyond providing a safe place on which to depend to helping Ruth regain, on a more ego-syntonic basis, a sense of competency and autonomy. Otherwise, she would merely repeat her experiences in the neuropsychiatric unit and with her outpatient psychiatrist, wherein she depends on someone else and experiences herself as powerless. The issue is not merely to be a better therapist than were her psychiatrists, but to help her grow her own autonomy, sense of reality, and ability to challenge authority which does not seem to be acting in her best interests.

Alleviation of Ruth's suffering, as well as prevention for other women, involves three foci. Girls and women need to be taught to value their autonomy and self-knowledge so that they don't grow up to feel so dependent on others who can power-fully mis-advise or misuse them, and so that they don't regress or decompensate when they move out of a supportive environment. Indeed, a new definition of femininity, based on strength, competence, authenticity, and wholeness must continue to evolve. The medical establishment must be re-educated to approach women patients seriously and not dismiss many of their complaints as psychosomatic and in need of tranquilizing. People in extremely stressful, away-from-home situations like war could benefit from the creation of support/discussion groups to offer a supportive "family" environment. These groups would provide contexts for anticipating and dealing with psychological trauma before and as it is happening, before it has a chance to elaborate itself into major disintegrative phenomena. This is also relevant to women generally. Women typically create and value relationships, communities, and networks of caring. The male establishment tends to see this as dependent and undifferentiated, but a feminist orientation views this connectedness as necessary to provide support and emotional nourishment.

As women regard themselves, their needs, and their perceptions of their life experiences as valid, they will not tolerate the kinds of shoddy, condescending malpractice and mistreatment rampant in their attempts to deal with their life problems. This applies not only in relation to the medical profession, but as we deal with our life issues and the interface of these with the myriad of people, agencies, and facilities with which we are all inter-dependent. Women who believe in their own worth and their own reality cannot be so susceptable to abusive, dependent relationships and to intense self-doubt and lack of sense of reality. As a woman's psychology evolves and as women explore and share their experiences and their sense of reality, this personal and archetypal validation will strengthen women individually and universally as being fully functional, autonomous individuals who know and trust themselves.

REFERENCES

Bolen, J.S., (1984). *Goddesses in Everywoman*. San Francisco: Harper & Row.

Davis, M., & Wallbridge, D., (1981). *Boundary and Space*. New York: Brunner-Mazel Publishers.

Eichenbaum, L., & Orbach, S., (1983). *Understanding Women*. New York: Coward-McCann, Inc.

Gilligan, C., (1982). *In a Different Voice*. Cambridge, MA: Harvard University Press.

Miller, J.B., (1976). *Toward a New Psychology of Women*. New York: Beacon Press.

Peele, S., & Brodsky, A., (1975). *Love and Addiction*. New York: Signet.

Scarf, M., (1980). *Unfinished Business*. Garden City, N.Y.: Doubleday & Company.

Shapiro, D., (1983). *Neurotic Styles*. New York: Basic Books, Inc.

The Diagnostic Approach:
The Usefulness of the DSM-III
and Systematic Interviews
in Treatment Planning

Karen John

INTRODUCTION

Despite continuing controversy in the mental health professions regarding the validity and clinical utility of the categorical classification of signs and symptoms of psychological disturbances (and even regarding the broad concept of "mental illness") the nosological approach to diagnosis in psychiatry is becoming increasingly influential. Both public and private agencies require the assignment of diagnoses based on the application of criteria contained in the American Psychiatric Association's *Diagnostic and Statistical Manual, 3rd Edition* (DSM-III) (APA Task Force on Nomenclature and Statistics, 1980), and private practitioners, whose clients depend on third party payments for their treatment, must also consult the DSM-III and assign conforming diagnoses. Furthermore, the Federal Government has undertaken a number of studies that are examining the differential efficacy of a variety of treatments for specified DSM-III diagnoses (e.g. depression, anxiety disorders, alcohol and substance abuse), in order to deter-

Karen John is an Associate in Research for the Depression Research and Clinical Methodology Units, Department of Psychiatry, Yale University School of Medicine. She has played a major role in the design and conduct of the Depression Research Unit's longitudinal study of the children of major depressives and normal controls. She has been a consultant to NIMH on the assessment of DSM-III, Axis II personality disorders and to a number of other projects concerned with the psychosocial and diagnostic assessment of children and adults.

Work on this paper was supported in part by the Yale Mental Health Clinical Research Center, grant MH30929, and the John P. and Catherine T. MacArthur Foundation Network on Risk and Protective Factors in the Major Mental Disorders.

91

mine the most effective and least expensive treatment methods, and ultimately to increase accountability among mental
health care providers. All of these recent developments suggest that no clinician—regardless of her acceptance or rejec-
tion of the theoretical basis of the diagnostic system contained
in the DSM-III—can escape its use.

Although I have no real evidence for asserting that women
working in the mental health professions are less favorably
disposed to the nosological diagnostic approach reflected in
the DSM-III, the fact that women in the field are more likely
to be psychologists, social workers, counselors or nurses—
disciplines that traditionally focus on the role of social factors
in psychological disturbance and a dimensional concept of
mental health—probably contributes to what I have observed:
that greater numbers of women question the authority and
value of the DSM-III. Because I believe that the DSM-III can
serve as a useful guide in the evaluation and treatment of
clients, and that women clinicians may have only a cursory
knowledge of it, or may feel ambivalent or hostile toward it, I
will first say something about the design and development of
the DSM-III and structured diagnostic interviews that generate prespecified (e.g., DSM-III) diagnoses, and then I will
attempt to show in my relatively brief discussion of Ruth's
case history how comfort with and a fuller understanding of
the DSM-III can lead to an earlier and more accurate assessment of a client's difficulties, and as a result, to more appropriate and effective treatment.

THE DESIGN AND DEVELOPMENT
OF THE DSM-III

The DSM-III diagnostic scheme is best viewed as a tenta-
tive and largely atheoretical system that provides clinicians
and researchers with a common language and framework with
which to communicate about and study the disorders for
which they have professional responsibility. The final version
of the Manual was regarded by its authors as ". . . only one
still frame in the ongoing process of attempting to better un-

derstand mental disorders" (APA Task Force on Nomenclature and Statistics, 1980, p. 12). To the extent that it was possible, the DSM-III criteria were based on up-to-the-minute clinical, epidemiological, family-genetic and biochemical data that supported the construct validity of the diagnostic categories that were included. But in keeping with the notion that the DSM-III represents an evolving diagnostic system, the Task Force has continued to meet and review evidence for revising the categories and criteria.

While it might be argued that the nosological approach to the diagnosis of disorder is not atheoretical, but rather betrays a disease concept—or the application of the "medical model"—in the identification and treatment of emotional disturbances, the members of the Task Force took great pains to adopt a primarily *descriptive* approach in formulating the diagnostic categories of mental disorders. For the most part, the descriptive approach avoids positing assumptions about the etiology of a disorder or syndrome, and instead focuses on clinical manifestations of the disturbance. It is in this sense that the DSM-III system of diagnosis is atheoretical. Theories about the causes or origins of the major mental disorders abound and are hotly debated, but the origins of most disorders are still unknown. DSM-III field trials indicated that clinicians can agree on the identification of disorders on the basis of their clinical manifestations without agreeing on how the disturbances come about (APA Task Force on Nomenclature and Statistics, 1980, p. 7).

The DSM-III contains descriptions of and criteria for the diagnosis of virtually every emotional and nonemotional mental disorder that has been found to be reliably identifiable by American mental health professionals. Only reliable and clinically useful diagnostic categories were included (Spitzer, Forman & Nee, 1979). An effort was made to ensure that categories and criteria were acceptable to clinicians and researchers of varying theoretical orientations, and that the diagnostic terms that appear in the DSM-III were familiar to most clinicians and were well-defined and consistently used throughout the manual.

The DSM-III employs a multiaxial diagnostic system: all of the mental disorders are coded on Axis I or II, and physical conditions, psychosocial stressors and the highest level of adaptive functioning within the year prior to the onset of disorder are coded on Axes III, IV and V, respectively. Personality and specific developmental disorders are listed on Axis II, and all other mental disorders and conditions are listed on Axis I. The DSM-III permits the concurrent diagnosis of multiple disorders on Axes I and II, and while diagnostic hierarchies are reflected in the exclusion criteria for specific disorders, the hierarchical conventions may be ignored if a clinician believes that noting the concomitant disorder adds important information to the diagnostic and treatment formulations. In fact, a recent family-genetic study of major depression, which was reported in the literature after the publication of the DSM-III, presented persuasive evidence for diagnosing specific anxiety disorders (generalized anxiety, panic, phobic and obsessive-compulsive disorders) when criteria for them are met, whether the symptoms of the anxiety disorder are associated with or are separate from episodes of depression (Leckman et al., 1983). The study showed that the first-degree relatives of former patients with major depression and an anxiety disorder (whether it occurred in conjunction with or separate from the episode of major depression) were 2–3 times more likely to have had major depression and anxiety disorders than the first-degree relatives of former patients with major depression only and the first-degree relatives of control subjects with no history of psychological disturbance. These family data provide support for an "anxious" subtype of major depression, and in conjunction with pharmacologic data that suggest that persons with "anxious depressions" require different medication than persons with depression only, have led to a revision of the exclusion criteria for the anxiety disorders by the DSM-III Task Force. These changes will be reflected in the DSM-III, Revised Edition.

The above illustrates the dynamic process that is inherent in the DSM-III system. On the one hand it provides well-defined criteria for arriving at diagnoses, and on the other it encourages the ongoing evaluation of those criteria. It is up to the clinicians and researchers who treat and study persons with psychological disturbances to inform their colleagues and the DSM-III Task Force of their observations and findings regarding the limitations, usefulness and validity of the categories and criteria.

Structured Diagnostic Interviews

A major impetus in the development of the DSM-III was the success of the Research Diagnostic Criteria (RDC) (Spitzer, Endicott, and Robins, 1978) and the Schedule for Affective Disorders and Schizophrenia (SADS) (Endicott and Spitzer, 1978) in greatly increasing the reliability of diagnostic procedures. Earlier editions of the Diagnostic and Statistical Manual did not contain explicit inclusion and exclusion criteria for psychiatric diagnoses, which resulted in clinicians and researchers applying their own concepts and criteria to the disorders listed in the manuals. In order to reduce *criterion variance* in clinical settings and research studies, the RDC, which contain criteria for the diagnoses of most (Axis I) major mental disorders, were developed. Another source of unreliability in diagnosis is *information variance:* clinicians often have different amounts and kinds of information about those who come for treatment, and the questions that are asked in an intake interview vary from clinician to clinician and from patient to patient. The SADS is a semi-structured diagnostic interview that was designed to systematically collect information on the disorders covered by the RDC, and thereby reduce information variance in psychiatric diagnosis.

The DSM-III, like the RDC, contains explicit inclusion and exclusion criteria for psychiatric diagnosis, and nearly all of the diagnostic categories covered by the RDC appear in the DSM-III unchanged or with only minor alterations (Williams and Spitzer, 1982). Unfortunately, the DSM-III was not published with a companion interview, *and too often the question that might lead to an unsuspected and more accurate diagnostic evaluation does not get asked in the intake interview.* Interviews like the SADS and the more recent Structured Clinical Interview for DSM-III (SCID) (Spitzer and Williams, 1983) provide clinicians and researchers with a standardized and systematic method for inquiring about a person's current and past episodes of emotional disturbance. And again, regardless of the basic treatment or research orientation of the inquirer, the comprehensive coverage of these interviews are invaluable aids in planning treatment or in evaluating a person's appropriateness for a given study. Both the SADS and the SCID are criterion-based interviews that are arranged by diagnostic category: a screening question for each category is asked, and if the screening criterion is met, additional questions within the section are asked; if the screening criterion is not met, the section is skipped. A complete SADS or SCID interview takes a clinically trained interviewer from 1 1/2 to 2 hours to complete (depending on the degree of disturbance) and generates RDC or DSM-III diagnoses for most of the Axis I major mental disorders and for some Axis II disorders. If either interview is to be used in research, potential interviewers should receive formal training, and interrater reliability should be assessed prior to study conduct and periodically throughout the study to ascertain interviewer "drift." An acceptable level of interrater reliability can be achieved in 8–15 hours of training.

The Importance of Diagnosis in Treatment Planning

As I suggested earlier, the primary purpose of interviewing and assigning diagnoses to persons who come for help is to provide therapists with information that is often essential in planning treatment. Diagnoses serve as shorthand descriptors of psychological disturbances, which when conventionally used make it possible for therapists to draw on the clinical and research experience of others. Information about the kinds of treatment that have proven to be most effective, ineffective or even harmful for persons with a given set of symptoms can only be accessed and applied if a common descriptive language is used. For example, if a therapist discovers in an interview that a person who is suffering from melancholic major depression has experienced in the past periods of marked irritability and other symptoms of hypomania, she will be alerted to a possible diagnosis of bipolar disorder. The therapist may be aware (from her own experience, from the literature—e.g., Weissman, 1983—or from her colleagues) that a combination of tricyclic antidepressants and psychotherapy has been found to be the most effective treatment for endogenous (melancholic) major depression; she may also be aware—or she might discover articles in the literature on the treatment of bipolar disorder— that persons with bipolar illness who are given tricyclics for depression often switch rapidly into hypomanic or manic states and drop out of treatment (e.g., Depue et al., 1981).

RUTH'S DIAGNOSIS AND TREATMENT

Anyone who is familiar with the DSM-III criteria for post-traumatic stress disorder (PTSD) would not hesitate in assigning that Axis I diagnosis to Ruth. From the case description, there is no doubt that: A. *a recognizable stressor that would evoke significant symptoms of distress in almost everyone* existed for Ruth; B. (1) she reexperienced the event through *recurrent and intrusive recollections,* (2) *recurrent dreams,* and (3) *sudden acting or feeling as if the traumatic event were recurring;* C. *numbing of responsiveness* and *reduced involvement with the external world* began for Ruth *some time after the trauma as shown by-* (1) *markedly diminished interest in one or more significant activities,* (2) *feeling detached and estranged from others,* and (3) *constricted affect;* and D. (1) *hyperalertness,* (2) *sleep disturbance,* (3) *guilt about surviving* (as evidenced in the theme of her dreams), (5) *avoidance of activities that aroused recollection of the traumatic event,* and (6) *intensification of symptoms by exposure to events that symbolize or resemble the traumatic event* were all part of Ruth's symptom picture. In short, not only did Ruth meet DSM-III criteria for PTSD, she had all but one of the possible symptoms listed: (D.4) memory *impairment or trouble concentrating* was not mentioned in the case description, but had she been asked, may well have been found to be experienced by her. In addition, Ruth's alcohol abuse/dependence would be diagnosed (as clearly secondary to PTSD) on Axis I. Ruth's self-mutilating behavior, lability, and poor social functioning might suggest an Axis II, personality diagnosis if considered out of context, but the presence of PTSD and her premorbid social adjustment would make such a diagnosis unlikely.

What is horrifying about Ruth's case from a diagnostic standpoint (not to mention from a *human* one, when confronted with prolonged and seemingly needless suffering) is that she spent four years in treatment with a psychiatrist who seems to have completely ignored the evidence of her PTSD and treated her as an hysteric with conversion symptoms. PTSD is one of the few disorders that appears in the DSM-III for which a known and unequivocal stressor is required. Furthermore, PTSD is not a *new* diagnostic category (see Horowitz, 1976), and anxiety, depressive, alcohol and substance abuse disorders are often associated with it and may also be diagnosed and treated. It would seem that anyone treating a veteran who is in distress about war experiences would consider the diagnosis of PTSD and find out what she could about others' knowledge of the manifestations and treatment of the condition.

It is well-documented in the literature that persons with PTSD often eschew treatment, and that when they do go they may avoid revealing information that would lead to a correct diagnosis (Horowitz, 1976). Neither was true of Ruth; she sought treatment and according to the case description, was willing to discuss her PTSD symptoms. Most clinicians who have treated and studied persons with PTSD agree that treatment should deal directly with the memories of the traumatic event (Horowitz et al., 1976). In order to give Ruth's original therapist the benefit of the doubt, I scanned the early literature on PTSD to discover the types of treatment that had been recommended around the time that Ruth first sought help. With little effort I found that in 1965 Archibald et al., who conducted a twenty-year follow-up study of World War II veterans suffering from chronic "combat fatigue," passionately argued that such persons should be encouraged to abreact their experiences—preferably with a group of individuals who have undergone a similar trauma. They further argued that since the passage of time served only to bring additional victims to treatment after two decades of trying to "forget it," and that since it appeared that changes incident to age exacerbate their problems, early case identification and treatment designed to facilitate working through the experiences should be pursued energetically by the mental health community.

SUMMARY

The DSM-III provides clinicians and researchers with categories and criteria for the diagnosis of nearly every emotional and nonemotional mental disorder that has been found to be reliably identifiable and clinically useful in the American mental health professions. Increasingly, clinicians in public and private agencies are required to assign DSM-III diagnoses to those who come for treatment, and even private practitioners are asked to do so when their clients depend on third party payments. I attempted to show that if the DSM-III diagnostic scheme is viewed as an evolving system that enables clinicians to communicate in a common language about the disturbances that are manifest in those who come to them for help, it serves as a useful tool in both formulating a treatment plan for an individual client and in furthering our understanding of the disorders that people experience. Diagnostic interviews that are designed to generate DSM-III criteria are other useful tools in the evaluation of clients, in that they ensure that the information that a clinician obtains about a client's current and past emotional problems is reasonably comprehensive, and that conditions that might otherwise be overlooked do not go undetected. Regardless of a clinician's theoretical orientation, obtaining information systematically from a client and arriving at a diagnostic assessment that is comparable to assessments made by others puts the clinician in touch with a large body of information about complications, differential diagnoses and treatment approaches specific to a disorder with which she may have little or no prior experience.

REFERENCES

American Psychiatric Association Task Force on Nomenclature and Statistics (1980). *Diagnostic and Statistical Manual of Mental Disorders, 3rd Edition.* Washington, D.C.: American Psychiatric Association.

Archibald, H. C. & Tuddenham, R. O. (1965). Persistent stress reaction after combat: A 20–year follow–up. *Arch Gen Psychiat., 12,* 475–481.

Depue, R. A., Slater, J. F., Wolfstetter–Kausch, H., Klein, D., Goplerud, E. & Farr, D. (1981). Behavioral paradigm for identifying persons at risk for bipolar depressive disorder: A conceptual framework and five validation studies. *J. Abnor. Psychol. Monogr., 90,* 381–437.

Endicott, J. & Spitzer R. L. (1978). A diagnostic interview: The Schedule for Affective Disorders and Schizophrenia. *Arch Gen Psychiat., 35,* 837–844.

Horowitz, M. J., (1976). *Stress Response Syndromes.* New York: Jason Aronson.

Leckman, J. F., Merikangas, K. R., Pauls, D. L., Prusoff, B. A., & Weissman, M. M. (1983). Anxiety disorders and depression: Contradictions between family study data and DSM–III conventions. *Am. J. Psychiat., 140,* 880–882.

Spitzer, R. L., Endicott, J. & Robins, E. (1978). Research Diagnostic Criteria: Rationale and reliability. *Arch. Gen. Psychiat., 35,* 773–782.

Spitzer, R. L., Forman, J. B. W., & Nee, J. (1979). DSM–III field trials: I. Initial interrater diagnostic reliability. *Am. J. Psychiat., 136,* 815–817.

Spitzer, R. L., & Williams, J. B. W. (1985). *Structured Clinical Interview for DSM–III—Patient Version* (SCID–P, 3/1/85). New York State Psychiatric Institute.

Weissman, M. M. (1983). Pharmacotherapy and psychotherapy for ambulatory depression: Efficacy and choices. In M. H. Greenhill & A. Gralnick (Eds.), *Psychopharmacology and Psychotherapy* (pp. 37–52). New York: The Free Press.

Williams, J. B. W. & Spitzer, R. L. (1982). RDC and DSM–III: An annotated comparison. *Arch. Gen. Psychiat., 39,* 1283–1289.

Perspectives of a Pastoral Counselor

Beth Adamson

WHAT IS PASTORAL COUNSELING?

The areas of focus, techniques, and resources which I utilize as a Pastoral Counselor are not unlike the approach of any "secular" therapist. One might ask why Pastoral Counseling exists at all and what such a discipline uniquely offers that can augment the field of therapies. Priests and ministers have been in the heart of communities of believers for centuries. It is not surprising that a process of evolution has occurred in response to the needs of the flesh and blood people that incorporate a congregation.

Throughout the years, as our definition of external demons has been reinterpreted as internal neuroses and psychoses, it is natural that the roles, techniques, and styles of the clergy would follow suit. Exorcism has been replaced in most cases by a psychological understanding of internal suffering, and appropriate means of healing have been sought. The stern, austere Father/Mother Confessor have, for the most part, evolved into a compassionate source of concern for persons experiencing grief, guilt, and pain. The Spiritual Director has moved from strictly directing a person through routinized spiritual exercises to guiding a seeker's internal growth in an approach which responds to and balances her or his emotional and spiritual needs.

The clergy find themselves in a prime position to observe the emotional and relational needs of members of their congregation, and seek out skills, resources, and "specialists" to deal with these needs. In my own survey of various ministers

Beth Adamson, M.A.R., Yale Divinity School, is affiliated with the United Methodist Church, in service to non-institutionalized ministry. She is currently a management consultant for many Fortune 500 corporations. She lives in West Redding, Connecticut, with her husband and their two daughters.

in the southern New England area in which I live, each estimates that they spend approximately 30–40% of their workweek counseling individuals, couples and families from their community. Even persons outside a specific congregation frequently seek out a minister as a trustworthy source of guidance and healing.

Clebsch and Jaekle (1964) have identified the four functions of pastoral care as healing, sustaining, guiding, and reconciling; and Howard Clinebell (1966) suggests that each function has changed significantly in the life of the church. The area of healing has emerged from "anointing, exorcism, and charismatic healing" to in-depth counseling and spiritual growth. The function of sustaining has moved from consoling and overseeing recuperation to supportive and/or crisis counseling. Guiding is no longer advice-giving and devil-craft, but educative counseling, decision-making and marital care. And the reconciling acts, which once were made up of confession-forgiveness and discipline now include confrontational counseling, existential counseling, and family therapy.

As the need has emerged for pastors to become counselors, the door has opened for a specialty field. Most seminaries offer, and many denominations "highly recommend" that any pastor moving into a people-oriented or "parish" community take part in a formalized Clinical Pastoral Education program, which supervises experiences in chaplaincy, counseling and group dynamics. Within the past three decades, the American Association of Pastoral Counselors has arisen, overseeing the study and practice of the specialty and publishing literature in the field.

Large congregations, able to afford a staff of clergy, will often appropriate funds for a full-time pastor whose primary role is counseling. Pastoral Counseling Centers are springing up, often supported by several churches in a particular community, neighborhood, or within one specific denomination in a designated area. And, as in my case, a community mental health center, treatment program, or agency may choose to incorporate a Pastoral Counselor in their inter-disciplinary staff.

While the discipline of Pastoral Counseling may differ little from other therapies, people often designate such therapists as "keepers of the soul." Most Pastoral Counselors, while they will not press the subject unbidden by the client, are indeed attentive to the spiritual aspect of an individual's psyche . . . their "heart of hearts."

PASTORAL COUNSELING FOR RUTH

The first question I ponder when a woman like Ruth presents herself to me is: "Why has this person come to me at this time?" Is Ruth aware that I'm a Pastoral Counselor, and does she understand what that means? Are her issues laced with religious conflicts, perhaps, so that my theological understanding is needed? Or, has she come because I am a woman and a feminist? Or, perhaps she seeks a style of therapy which tends to be supportive, nurturing, and non-traditional?

My first consideration in assessing a potential client is whether there is a good match between Ruth's needs and at least some of my skills. That assessment would include an honest evaluation of what I don't offer, for while Pastoral Counseling is described as being a relational, supportive, ego-adaptive, and reality-oriented approach to therapy (Clinebell, 1966), I don't pretend to provide in-depth psycho-analytic expertise.

What I can do is to "minister" to a fellow human in an approach that is as egalitarian as possible. In an effort to downplay the idea of "professional" versus "client," the setting is symbolic. No sterile atmosphere here, as the therapy would probably take place in the study of my home, with my little girl nearby, upstairs or outdoors under the supervision of a sitter. Ruth is invited into my environment—not removed to an isolated office space or hospital-type setting reserved for the emotional deviants of society. A model is provided and an expectation set up for functional behavior— and due attention would be paid to Ruth's reaction. Is the home and family setting motivational and trust-building or does it incite anxiety? Such feelings and issues would be discussed and processed.

As a pastor and a feminist, I have a theological understanding, a religious education, and a feminist awareness which affords me the opportunity for insights into the cultural backdrop of Ruth's upbringing. The Judeo-Christian heritage is often targeted as the root of the white male system, but in this "modern age," we sometimes underplay the severity of the anti-feminine sentiment implicit in the tradition. Young girls, however, often catch that message and incorporate it into their self-understanding. Castelleja (1973, p. 88) has termed this the "imp" in every woman: "the one who tells her that she is no good." A former client of mine, not unlike Ruth in her Roman Catholic upbringing and various life experiences which led to self-mutilation and suicidal behavior, was particularly articulate about her childhood interpretations of church teachings. She wrote in her journal:

> It was through a woman that mankind fell into Original Sin, so every woman must bear the Original Sin of Eve. No woman can really be good except for Mary the Mother of Jesus. All other women have no chance to be anything but evil.

Is it to similar internal messages in Ruth that I must "minister"?

In Ruth's life, the old model of confession and forgiveness (to the male priest behind closed doors) may need to metamorphose onto an open discussion. With support and caring, we can explore Ruth's feelings of self-deprecation, uncovering their origins in her personal history. We can also look at and understand the part a chauvinistic male structure played in reinforcing that negative image—guiding the interaction to a point of closure which is not unlike the forgiveness experience.

Another aspect of my training is to understand Ruth, not as an isolated individual—but as a member of a social structure that includes everyone she would incorporate in her personal history. Thus, even if overt ties have been cut off with many family members, the male with whom she had sexual relations, the psychologist and doctors who had misdiagnosed her, and particularly those servicepersons (living and dead) whom she treated in Viet Nam, we would explore their roles in her self-understanding. We would certainly discuss her feelings and/or sense of isolation from those people currently in her social network. If Ruth expressed the need, I would provide the opportunity to include individuals (family or friends) in conjoint sessions, and I would encourage any potential interfacing with members of her AA group or VA aftercare group.

But, perhaps more importantly, Ruth seems to have issues of grief, possible anger or guilt, and lack of closure with many people who are no longer available to her (due to separation or death). In such areas, I have the utmost respect for gestalt therapies and psychodrama as techniques to help Ruth explore such feelings and relationships with my guidance. Should Ruth decide that she would like help resolving issues with selected people and events from her past, I would probably call upon help and guidance from colleagues within these disciplines to support my efforts. It is perhaps a unique trait of Pastoral Counseling that, as integral members of a community, we have access to a variety of professional colleagues who can augment our skills, and trained to know our weaknesses, we openly seek out their guidance and consultation.

Dreamwork would also be important, and I would suggest that Ruth record each dream she remembers—good or bad. In the same journal, I would suggest she include descriptions of the various hallucinations, treating them as symbolic messages to herself not unlike (and not much more unusual) than her dreams. Some of these dreams might become the material which serves as a springboard for psychodramas, etc.

Ruth's sexuality, likewise, will not be ignored. As her experience with males has been minimal and more negative than positive, I might suggest that she join a women's sexuality group to enable her to explore her own sexual history in light of other women's experience—while also providing support and options in the exploration of her self, her body, and her sexual needs. Work with other women also provides the opportunity for Ruth to look at stereotypically female issues, their origins, and alternatives. Assertiveness is one such issue. As is the "need" to nurture, with the accompanying resentment women frequently experience. Ruth's experience second-mothering her little sister, as well as her call to become a nurse may fall into such a category. Another benefit of a women's group is the intimacy and support such a group potentially provides, which might give Ruth more in-depth caring and interconnectedness than she has apparently experienced thus far in her other therapy groups.

If sought, guidance and care can be provided for questions

of the spirit. Feelings—good, bad, or questioning—about God can be openly discussed. And prayer and meditation are seen as valid routes to growth, utilizing silence, appropriate readings, and/or scripture. With great care, a conscientious Pastoral Counselor works to avoid "preaching" her own interpretation and understanding of theology in an effort to guide any "seeker" to an experience of faith which is wholly theirs. Perhaps hidden within the fabric of Ruth's suffering is a dimension of grief, fear of mortality, or anxiety about death which draws her to pastoral counseling.

And it is to this, perhaps, that I could guide Ruth in time, helping her, as the theologian Paul Tillich says: "to encounter the dimension of ultimate concern" (1963). And perhaps in the quiet, caring guidance of such a discipline she can find the grace to become whole.

REFERENCES

Claremont de Castelleja, I. (1973). Knowing Woman. New York, NY: Harper & Row.
Clebsch, W, & Jaekle, C. (1964). Pastoral Care in Historical Perspective. Englewood Cliff, NJ: Prentice-Hall.
Clinebell, H. (1966). Basic Types of Pastoral Counseling. Nashville, TN: Abingdon Press.
Tillich, P. (1963). Address, National Conference of Clinical Pastoral Education. Atlantic City, NJ.

Propping Up the Patriarchy: The Silenced Soldiering of Military Nurses

Joy A. Livingston
Joanna M. Rankin

The armed forces may get nervous when nurses start telling their stories because they reveal so much about the nature of war itself. Not only the military gender structure is being protected by military nurses' silence; the basic legitimacy of the military as a pillar of civilized society is being protected by their silence. A nurse who *talks* of war as seen from a military hospital or a MASH unit is a dangerous woman.

Cynthia Enloe, 1983

Authors' Note: We have been developing an analysis of militarism from a feminist perspective. Feminism, in its essence, is a critique of patriarchal power and a model for a new kind of power. The patriarchy defines power as control over, as dominance, and this is clearly manifested in militarism. Militarism, like any form of dominant power, is based on dualistic thinking, assuming that some people are better than others, thus

Joy A. Livingston, Ph.D., is a member of the Burlington Women's International League for Peace and Freedom, Co-convenor of Burlington Women's Council, feminist activist and Burlington College staff member, where she coordinates Student Support Services and teaches Women's Studies courses. (Ph.D. in Psychology from University of Vermont, B.A. in Psychology from University of California at Los Angeles.)

Joanna M. Rankin, Ph.D., is a member of the Burlington Women's International League for Peace and Freedom, feminist activist and Associate Professor of Astronomy in the Physics Department of the University of Vermont where she represents Eco-feminist approaches to the study and practice of Science. (Ph.D. in Astrophysics from the University of Iowa, M.S. from Tulane University, and B.S. from Southern Methodist University.)

justifying hierarchical and violent control over those who are seen as less valuable. The goal of dominant models, particularly militarism, is to win, not to resolve conflict. Indeed, dominants avoid any open exposure of the actual basis of conflicts, thus both preventing problem resolution and hiding the structure of dominant power.

In contrast, feminism offers a model that defines power from within, as choice. In this cooperative model, unlike the dominant model, the assumption is that all people are of equal value and importance, and that relationships are built on each person's right to choose. The goal is to promote a high quality of life, not death in the pursuit of winning.

We focus on militarism as a manifestation of dominant patriarchal power because militarism legitimizes patriarchal power, particularly the use of violence to dominate and control. Moreover, women are coerced and persuaded to collaborate with the military since our participation is essential to the continuation of the military institution. In a dominant power structure the true nature of conflicts is hidden, and so the military is not always recognized as a system for domestic control as much as a protection against external threats.

Based on this feminist analysis of militarism, we discussed Ruth's case study. Excerpts of our conversation follow:

Joanna: As a military nurse treating soldiers in combat zones, Ruth was absolutely essential to the conduct of the war. Military ideology, however, treats all women as irrelevant. So, Ruth is in the paradoxical position of being used by the military as a nurse, but marginalized and devalued as a woman.

Joy: Not one of her colleagues would discuss feelings about working in a war zone. When Ruth initially had an actual physical ailment it was attributed to a psychosomatic disorder. She was actively discouraged in psychotherapy from discussing her experiences in Viet Nam. This happened over and over again. She finally began therapy not convinced that her symptoms were real.

Joanna: Absolutely. It looks like she has no support whatsoever. Furthermore, there's a long history in the military of denying that women have anything to do with combat. The propaganda, both inside and outside of the military, is that women are there for "a lark," to have romantic adventures, and that their role has nothing to do with the real thing because that's what men do. But ever since World War II there has been less of a distinction between the "front" (where men are) and the "rear" (where women are said to be). The whole function of MASH (*m*obile *a*rmy *s*urgical *h*ospital) units is to put nurses and doctors as close to combat as possible. Women's experience in war then, as nurses, becomes as powerful, and as potentially destructive, as the kinds of combat experiences men have, but it is never admitted.

Joy: Yes, we cannot have women in combat, because they are thought incapable of coping. That is consistent with denying reality because then we can continue in the "phallacy" that things are operating according to the expressed plan. In the same way, war is considered just a response to unusual circumstances when, in fact, war is, and always has been, an integral part of patriarchal social structure. But this is not explicitly admitted.

Joanna: Women are essential to warfare. It is an old truth that women have great power to limit and end men's wars, but more frequently women have been drawn into participation in war as military wives, as workers in military industries, as mothers of sons, as military service workers, as military nurses, as paid or gratis recreation workers for soldiers such as prostitutes, as a reserve work force to replace men in civilian work, as well, of course, as actual combatants. Given that at least 10 support people are required for every actual soldier, it is women who make the military possible.

Joy: Of course, and this cannot be admitted. The validity of women's experience and their essential role is denied. And there seems to be a conspiracy of silence which keeps men men. If the reality were exposed, that women do have powerful combat experiences, then that would challenge the masculinity men earn by having combat experience.

Joanna: Women don't need to be associated with the military to prove that they are women. But men's masculinity, whether they are in the military or not, has some connection to military ideology. Masculinity is defined, for instance, in terms of "winning" and the capacity for violence (particularly in defense of the "good").

Joy: The military gives men a place to prove their masculinity. Proving masculinity involves proving that one is not a woman. So experiences that validate masculinity cannot be shared with women. That has a lot to do with the conspiracy of silence invalidating Ruth's experience, because her experience, her close experience of death and destruction, can't be acknowledged.

Joanna: A related issue is that male bonding is thought to facilitate the military institution. And so military commanders and leaders fear that if women's presence is acknowledged in the military sphere that it will undermine the bonding of men that makes men "good fighters" and is important to discipline, the chain of command, and the sense of adventure and dependence that makes the whole thing work. So women's presence is regarded as very dangerous. Women are always present, however. Because of this paradox their presence must be denied.

Joy: Exactly! And so Ruth's experience is totally invalidated. Meanwhile, you speak of how we are co-opted into supporting the military, and in so many ways I can see how Ruth has been co-opted. She was certainly well trained for thinking and acting hierarchically (i.e., patriarchally) being raised in a Catholic environment, and trained in the Naval nursing corp. Her method of coping with anything imposing on her is to isolate herself. In that way she fulfills an essential role, she cooperates with it by isolating herself when faced with problems rather than bonding with others and potentially threatening the structure. She was well trained to do that as well. It feels to me that power hierarchies need that kind of coping response.

Joanna: That is precisely what the military needs: women who can deal with the realities of being close to the front, of seeing horrible things, of being used and abused, of being marginalized, and cope with it personally.

Joy: Yes, all alone.

Joanna: All alone.

Joy: Otherwise they would be exposing their experience as a shared experience, as an actual experience.

Joanna: And it is completely off limits in the military for women to find support among themselves, to speak out, and to jointly authenticate their shared experience. That is really dangerous.

Joy: What amazes me, again and again, is that we treat all these forms of violence (wars, abuse, rape) as if they are abnormal. And I'm so struck by that because violence is hardly abnormal, but very normal, certainly not desirable, but normal and essential. The violence, both as physical violence and as the denial of choice, is vital to maintaining patriarchal structures. Here again is another denial, treating the normal as if it were abnormal.

Joanna: Indeed. About 3% of Viet Nam veterans are female, at least 7500 women, predominantly nurses, and many have protested the way they were treated by the Veteran's Administration (VA). As Cynthia Enloe says in *Does Khaki Become You?* (1983, p. 109) "When it uses the term 'Vietnam Veterans,' the VA usually means *male* veterans." Nurses struggle even to be recognized as suffering from combat-related illnesses such as post-traumatic stress disorder. The ideology is that women are not exposed to combat, but many nurses claim to have seen the worst of the Viet Nam war, "an endless procession of mangled bodies across the operating table" (p. 109). MASH units operate adjacent to combat zones and MASH units use women. Thus the denial that nurses are exposed to combat violence when, in fact, they are usually so exposed.

Joy: I'm struck by the irony of sending people out on purpose to get killed but making sure there is a medical unit nearby to save them. It would almost make more sense to let them get killed. What do you need with a medical unit? Isn't the point to kill each other?

Joanna: No, the point is to impose dominance. And from the military point of view, medical services make it possible to perpetuate the myth that the military has the best interests of its soldiers in mind.

Joy: So again it is another way of denying the truth. Medical services are for the morale of the soldiers.

Joanna: Yes, and one of the dangers of women's presence, and one of the reasons why the denial of women's experience is so important, is that if women spoke out about the realities of what is happening, if they found a voice that was credible, then there is the fear that their speaking out about the realities of warfare would undermine military activity.

Joy: Because they would expose the truth.

Joanna: They would expose the constructed lies about the situation.

Joy: Time and time again, women's experience is not validated. If it were it would threaten the patriarchal structure. Whenever women address our experiences of oppression by the patriarchy, we threaten to uncover the hidden bases of conflict. As Jean Baker Miller points out, in *Toward A New Psychology of Women* (1976), those in power, the dominants, need to believe everything is right and good just as it is, both for themselves and for the subordinates. So when we talk about these experiences of oppression and connect them and see them not as personalized, but as universally true for all subordinates, then we threaten to uncover the myth that keeps the system going. Of course it is incredibly threatening. Ruth, and the other nurses, are particularly threatening so they are even more severely abused and silenced.

Joanna: Ruth's personal tragedy is so intense. Obviously we can always see precursors to how she got into the situation, but the tragedy of her being there, presumably functioning very competently, and being denied, and trivialized, and marginalized, is just incredible. As Lynda Van Devanter, a Viet Nam nurse, points out in *Home Before Morning* (1983), there has historically been a fine line between being a military nurse and a prostitute. The presumption is that you sleep with soldiers. The long effort to professionalize military nursing has always struggled with the stigma that "you may be a professional, but we know what you really are." This circumstance affects the self esteem of military nurses. Furthermore, the women who served as nurses in Viet Nam, as did nurses in all wars, expected to do good, to care, to be useful, to be constructive, to save lives. But the sort of patients that Ruth saw, and that Lynda Van Devanter saw, were horribly maimed. Day by day, by the thousands. And (because the wounded were flown out as soon as possible) they never saw a patient recover. So if you are used to personalizing, you began to feel very ineffective about what you most care about doing. You don't criticize the system. The men learned sooner and better in Viet Nam that it wasn't that they were bad soldiers, it was a bad war, and it wasn't their fault. The women took a lot longer to learn this, and paid horrible tolls for personalizing their situation, however communally experienced.

Joy: Personalizing is a process well suited for being a cooperative part of that structure. The personal tragedy of it is awful; I am overwhelmed when I consider the pain involved. Again, it makes sense to me that cogs in an oppressive wheel *have* to personalize.

Joanna: Yes, depersonalization is essential.

Joy: No, I meant personalization, taking it on as their own problem.

Joanna: Actually, both things happen. There's a great deal of depersonalization in the military, in the training of soldiers, which presumably carries over to nursing as well. If one takes any personal responsibility for all that is happening, the pain becomes too much to cope with, so there is distancing. That distancing is a huge source of guilt among people who define themselves as caring people.

Joy: Right, to be a caring person who doesn't care is incredibly difficult. I agree with you, that depersonalization, disconnecting, estrangement as Starhawk calls it in *Dreaming The Dark* (1982), is clearly not only something you have to do to survive, but the military knows it is necessary for you to function. So you are trained to disconnect. And again, never being able to talk about your feelings, about what you are seeing, is a powerful disconnection, as if you didn't have feelings. I think the military requires its soldiers and nurses to not have feelings.

Joanna: Absolutely, that seems to be in the way that men in the military behave. To some extent men are probably able to bond with other men who are their "buddies" in emotionally meaningful ways. But women don't have those supports. Women in the military don't have meaningful ways to bond with other women, or for that matter with men. And women who do share their feelings with other women, and give any depth or importance to such relationships, are dangerous to the military and will clearly be labelled lesbian, and will of course suffer a great deal of persecution for that. So homophobia operates strongly to isolate women as well. Given the small number of women and the proscriptions against meaningful relationships, it is frightening to think how isolated were women in the Viet Nam war.

Joy: Yes, very frightening. And also, the cooperation among men extends beyond the military itself. When Ruth went to psychotherapy, she was seeing a male psychiatrist who discouraged her from discussing her experiences in Viet Nam. I think all men are encouraged to cooperate with perpetuating the myth that war doesn't have powerful negative consequences. I think one of the powerful things about the Viet Nam war was that a lot of men didn't cooperate with that myth, and started talking about the negative consequences. If the military is a place for men to prove that they are men, there would need to be cooperation among men, both within and outside of the military.

Joanna: Discussions about the folkways of war stories point out that men rarely talk about their wartime experiences, period. And if they do, only to other people with war experiences. How many men in your life have you heard talk about war stories?

Joy: Only one once, and it wasn't really a war story.

Joanna: I've heard men talk very superficially sometimes.

Joy: I've never heard about what it is like on the battle field.

Joanna: No, not even after World War II did men openly talk about their combat experiences. There really seems to be a strong taboo against talking about military experiences. Isn't it incredible that this taboo should extend into therapy? Indeed, the therapy of a woman by a male therapist. Isn't that amazing?

Joy: It is a powerful taboo, at least in our class experience. It may be that open discussion of suffering is more taboo among the middle class.

Joanna: I think that it is worth noting and identifying as a taboo. And that war time experience wouldn't be regarded as relevant material in therapy is remarkable! It is indicative of how deeply ingrained militarism is in our culture. There is another point I think is relevant here, and that is the myth about how people behave in warfare. After World War II, for instance—a relatively "popular" war—it developed that perhaps as many as half the U.S. soldiers were so terrified that they were unable to ever fire their weapons.

Joy: You sure don't hear much about that.

Joanna: When things get bad a whole lot of men lose it entirely. But you don't hear about this.

Joy: I wonder if war stories are not shared because a lot of that fear would be exposed.

Joanna: Fear and all kinds of reactions, and it certainly wouldn't do much for the masculine image.

Joy: Truly, what good is a war story to promote male identity if the story is about "chickening out"? Another part of this is not acknowledging the pain of war. The 10th year anniversary of the Viet Nam war did not allow for the pain, I think. Only a few editorials have been written to indicate this, that the war was not a glorious thing to remember and feel good about, and that the war triggered painful memories which are difficult to cope with.

Joanna: This, I think, is always true, but the pain of Viet Nam has perhaps been even more acute. Maimed and crippled veterans have never been welcome participants in Veteran's Day parades, but the trauma of the Viet Nam War continues. There have, for instance, been more post-war casualties through veteran suicides (about 60,000) than from the actual fighting (some 57,000). Socially we don't want to know about this side of militarism. That's part of the taboo.

Joy: The taboo is against acknowledging that people come back in pieces. It is okay to come back dead.

Joanna: Safely dead.

Joy: Safely dead, but certainly not mutilated.

Joanna: And if you do, you are supposed to be quiet and brave. You are certainly not supposed to speak about it.

Joy: It is the silence. To me, these are the important tools of the patriarchy maintaining itself. Denial and silencing, keeping reality covered, are so central, are so crucial, they are such important tools. They are just as important as the threat of violence or violence itself. Violence, or the threat of violence, creates fear, and we are kept afraid so that we behave "appropriately", and that means keeping quiet. In order to keep the dominant structure intact, subordinates are supposed to keep quiet. Not to expose the paradoxes, not to expose the hypocrisies, not to expose the true violence, not to expose that violence is normal to the structure.

Joanna: That in a sense it *is* the structure.

Joy: The structure is violence. They are inseparable. Starhawk identifies violence as dominance, the denial of choice, and that clearly describes patriarchal structure. But all the familiar systems of change with the exception of feminist systems (and not all feminist systems) perpetuate dominance by perpetuating dominant power structures. Just look at our language, we talk about "winning," "fighting." Once again, it is reminiscent of changing "chick" to "woman." As long as we keep using dominant power words and using that kind of thinking we are not going to change anything, it is like integrating textbooks merely by coloring white faces black. It will just be the same thing, over again. We'll have women's armies. I don't want to be in an army. I don't want to *win* the *fight*.

Joanna: You want to *resolve* the *problem*.

Joy: Precisely.

Joanna: It seems so fundamentally part of human culture, so fundamentally a part of all I've experienced in my life, and indeed is a part of me, how do we begin to change it?

Joy: That's why I think about language. For me, at this point, change is so overwhelming. Language is a place to start. Language is a good way to raise consciousness and awareness. Mary Daly in *Gyn/Ecology* (1978) and *Pure Lust* (1984), talks about the importance of language. And she talks about the necrophilia of patriarchy, identifying its death-dealing words. Then she proposes words like "biophilia." Indeed, it seems that the strongest way not to cooperate with patriarchy is to affirm life and live it fully and completely. Laying down and dying is just helping it along, the whole system is death-dealing, that is what the military is all about. That is why it is a farce to have medical services at the "front." War is all about killing people. And the myth that it is not killing people is perpetuated by having nurses patch up dead bodies. And in order to keep those nurses going their feelings have to be killed off. It is all about killing. Killing the feeling, killing the validity of the experience, it is just death, death, death. And so not to cooperate is to affirm life.

Joanna: Exactly.

Joy: Talking about death-dealing, I also noted that during the time when Ruth was confronting her alcoholism she was actively suicidal. So here Ruth is doing it for them, killing herself. I see Ruth as painfully the victim of this necrophilial system.

Joanna: Which raises the question of how could we be helpful to Ruth, what would be our recommendations to alleviate her distress and prevent such distress for future generations?

Joy: Prevention is what I think of first, and I have a very simple answer, we have to get rid of militarism and the patriarchal system behind it. Band-aids will not work, anything less than a complete change in our basic assumptions and our social structure ultimately is a band-aid.

Joanna: But on a less global scale, what I would say to this question, the way I could be helpful to Ruth, would be to suggest support groups with women who had similar Viet Nam experiences. And I could suggest to her that her experiences had a political and patriarchal context, helping her to understand that she was a victim from A to Z. A total victim. And I would hope to help her heal herself and to find ways to actively use her experience to resist militarization.

Joy: An important part of the healing process for all of us who have been victims is to become not victim, to own our power and to learn to take action. I would want to help Ruth learn to own her power, and certainly help her find support. For me, support is about helping her find ways to totally validate her experience.

Joanna: And emphasizing that her experience is personal and crucial. She has stories to tell, and by virtue of the fact that they are so hard to tell, so painful to tell, so suppressed, they are precisely what must be heard, so as to avoid endless repetitions of this distress for future generations.

Joy: So, in fact, her power rests in no longer being silent.

Joanna: Yes.

Joy: For me, there is a very painful place around this question of an individual's pain and tragedy within the context of the oppressive social, political and economic structure. I want to deal with and alleviate the pain of the individual, and recognize that, to some extent, that is impossible. Yet, her pain, if expressed, shakes the system in vital ways. That's why I am not a therapist. I have worked with women who were abused and those women were so personalized in their pain, and I couldn't share with them a larger analysis that could have been more helpful. I know that there are those who can do that.

Joanna: But isn't that a fundamentally political circumstance, what might be called the "shame of the oppressed"? When people learn to identify with each other in their pain rather than let pain isolate them, then social revolution becomes possible.

Joy: So that is why the patriarchy denies our experience, and keeps us silent. As soon as we speak out and learn to share our experience, we threaten to change the world.

REFERENCES

Daly, M. (1978) *Gyn/Ecology: The Metaethics of Radical Feminism.* Boston, Ma.: Beacon Press.
Daly, M. (1984) *Pure Lust: Elemental Feminist Philosophy.* Boston, Ma.: Beacon Press.

Enloe, C. (1983) *Does Khaki Become You? The Militarization of Women's Lives.* Boston, Ma.: South End Press.

Miller, J. B. (1976) *Toward a New Psychology of Women.* Boston, Ma.: Beacon Press.

Starhawk (1982) *Dreaming the Dark: Magic, Sex and Politics.* Boston, Ma.: Beacon Press.

Van Devanter, L. (with C. Morgan) (1983) *Home Before Morning The Story of an Army Nurse in Vietnam.* New York, NY: Beaufort Books.

Response From "Ruth"

Esther D. Rothblum, Ph.D.
Ellen Cole, Ph.D.
Editors, Women & Therapy
Burlington, VT 05405

Dear Esther and Ellen,

Thank you for giving me the opportunity to be a part of this issue. The process of sharing my story, both through participation in this journal and in preparing myself to address a professional meeting last summer, has brought me new understanding, new feelings of self-worth, affirmation and a sense of belonging.

In a general response to all of the articles, I would like to make a few comments.

The basic structure of feminist therapy, which has involved my increasing awareness of my own power, sharing of information between my therapist and me, affirming my experiences and teaching me to know the interactions of my body and mind has been tremendously important to my own process.

Within this framework, the theoretical approach of several of the authors could have led, I believe, to the progress I have made to date.

I felt an overwhelming sense of acceptance from these authors. Their understanding of my pain touched and supported me. In reading, I vacillated between a sense of excitement about the quality of the insight and writing as I viewed the case of "Ruth" as detached from me; an urgent desire to fill in the blanks, to enlarge, to explain the "Ruth" that really is me; and a sense of wonder that people I had never met could so sensitively approach my story.

The real "Ruth" lives, breathes, and goes to AA meetings.

And, thanks in large part to two years of therapy, I was able to read these manuscripts with gratitude and joy.

I was, however, disappointed in Michelle Clark's article. Although she makes several good points, I feel many aspects of alcoholism in women were presented in "Ruth's" case discussion, and that expansion of these would have strengthened understanding of the disease.

My story is not terminally unique; I'm an alcoholic, I am a woman, I am a victim of "silenced trauma". In the course of my alcoholism recovery, I've learned that the majority of women alcoholics deal with issues, in a broad sense, identical to my own.

Today I see hundreds of women in the AA meetings I attend who can be described in this way. Many of these women have become close friends, sponsors and sponsorees.

In sharing our experience, strength and hope with one another, we also find we share many issues related to isolation, low self-esteem, depression, self-destructive behavior, trauma (incest, rape, battering, war), gender-role stereotyping, dysfunctional families, and poverty. Many of us need "outside help" as is recommended in *Alcoholics Anonymous,* the "big book" of the AA fellowship.

Alcoholism and other chemical dependencies occur in about 7–10% of the population. While women are, still, less often diagnosed and treated, it appears that the incidence of these diseases is the same for both men and women.

I would like to see a full issue of *Women & Therapy* devoted to alcoholism and women. Such a format would afford the opportunity to deal with these issues more appropriately and thoroughly.

Therapists dealing with Viet Nam veterans—female and male—may also want to be aware that issues such as Agent Orange exposure, disrupted work histories leading to financial problems and current events, including "pop" culture involving war and casualties (the Grenada invasion; Rambo) are likely to impact the way clients experience their present.

Like me, women who served in Viet Nam are now in their late thirties or early forties. I found it amusing, in reading some of the manuscripts, to see "Ruth" viewed by the authors as a very young woman.

You asked what life is like for me today. I *am* forty, I have, at this writing, over two years of sobriety, and am celebrating my second anniversary in therapy this month.

I've lived alone since returning to Seattle from California— and continue to do so, in my own home. So far, my house-keeping is adequate but not stellar. I decorate with book shelves.

I read voraciously; it's exciting to find that my mind works again, after ten years of alcoholic drinking. At any point in time, my "bibliotherapy" includes feminist thought and opinion, poetry, current and classical fiction and an assortment of journals, magazines and anthologies about psychology, alcoholism, science, home improvement and women's studies.

I continue to attend AA on a regular basis. During my first year of sobriety, "regular" meant nine meetings a week, as well as therapy with Laura Brown, peer-counseling at the Viet Nam Veterans Outreach Center, and aftercare at the VA Alcohol Treatment Program.

Today I go to three to five AA meetings a week, primarily women's meetings. I participate because I want to—AA is the foundation for my sobriety and my friends are there. I work the AA program, read the literature, have sponsors and am a sponsor myself.

Three years ago, I spent my evenings home, alone, watching television and drinking. Now, my life is full of activities with friends: hiking, camping, white-water rafting, lectures, concerts, and long and warm conversations over pots of good coffee.

My nightmares are fewer. Hallucinations still come, but not so often. Surrounded by the fellowship of AA and many people who love me, I still try to isolate, I struggle against urges to self-mutilate, and I run in fear of opportunities for intimacy. There is still work to do.

Several of the contributors to this journal anticipated that "Ruth" would experience problems in interpersonal relationships. Lorna Sarrel is particularly on-target for me with her discussion of how "Ruth" might experience herself as sexually inadequate.

In the process of my recovery, I have identified myself as a lesbian, and found that my early sexual experience, although heterosexual, still influences my relationships today. While not yet able to have sex without flashbacks, my openness to intimacy, love and friendship is growing daily—at a some-times frightening rate.

The other work I'm doing in therapy today includes identi-fying and "owning" myself as victim, experiencing and ex-pressing my anger (both old and new), and taking risks, through my fear, to ask for help, be close, be honest.

Still to come are more discoveries. I am a photographer, and my work improves and gives me joy. For the first time in ten years, I am returning to the classroom this quarter. I've registered for a writing class, feeling ready for a new way of sharing. It's exciting to be me; life *has* begun at forty.

Besides the personal benefits and growth opportunities I have gained through participating in this special issue, I feel a sense of hope for other women. There are still women in the military. They are still, predominantly, caregivers. The con-flict between the requirements of war and the imperatives of caring that I experienced, like my alcoholism, is not unique to "Ruth."

I have the feeling that not many women veterans of Viet Nam who need it are yet in treatment or therapy. I would welcome personal communication from anyone who is inter-ested.

I'm glad you've done this good work. Many Ruths and their therapists need to hear what all of you have to say.

love, and thank you,

"Ruth"